Praise for *Leading with Heart*

Too often, self-care, collective care and justice are seen as ill-matched threads that cannot be woven together. This well-researched and very readable book weaves together these threads in clear, instructive and helpful ways. The various authors show how care for self, care for the collective and care for justice are, in fact, not three separate threads, but the same thread seen from different perspectives. I heartily recommend this book.
- *Russ Moxley, Honorary Senior Fellow, Center for Creative Leadership*

Leading with Heart provides a significant contribution to the field of educational leadership by illuminating the intersection between intrapersonal wellness, justice, and flourishing systems of education. It provides a map of the inner resources necessary for inspired leadership—heart, vision, action, and wisdom while exploring the essential role of mindfulness in developing these capacities. Most importantly, it provides heartening stories of awareness, impact and transformation from those on the path of leadership development. This book is a must read for anyone interested in creating and sustaining caring, trustworthy educational environments where everyone belongs and everyone thrives.

Margaret Golden, EdD
Director of Forum for Educator Well-Being, Professor Emerita of Education

I highly recommend Leading With Heart as it provides readers with insight and strategies to practice mindfulness and self-care around the successes and challenges inherent in educational leadership.
Judith Sykes, Alberta. Principal, School Library Leader, Author – of late The Whole School Library Learning Commons: An Educators' Guide (Libraries Unlimited).

Leading with Heart

Enacting Self-Care, Collective Care, and Justice

Dr. Amy Burns
Dr. Mary-Ann Mitchell-Pellett

Foreword by Shelly L. Francis

Word & Deed Publishing Incorporated
1860 Appleby Line, Suite #778
Burlington, Ontario, Canada, L7L 7H7

Copyright © 2020 Word & Deed Publishing Incorporated

Leading with Heart
Enacting Self-Care, Collective Care, and Justice

All rights reserved. Except as permitted under (U.S. Copyright Act of 1976), or (Canadian Copyright Act of 2012), no part of this publication may be reproduced, distributed, or transmitted in any form or by any means, or stored in a database or retrieval system, without the prior written permission of the publisher.

Steve Viau, copyeditor
Book design by Jim Bisakowski – www.bookdesign.ca

ISBN 978-1-9994224-6-2

Word & Deed Publishing Incorporated
1860 Appleby Line, Suite #778
Burlington, Ontario, Canada, L7L 7H7
(Toll Free) 1-866-601-1213

Visit our website at
www.wordanddeedpublishing.com

Acknowledgements

There are many people who have had a hand in this volume and we wish to express our gratitude for their interest and guidance. First, thanks to the Werklund School of Education who initially provided research support, allowing the Leading with Heart program, and as such this volume, to come into being. Also, thanks very sincerely to Darrin Griffiths for his interest in and support of this volume. His patience and attention made the process both enjoyable and instructive. Finally, thanks to all our chapter authors, all of whom were students in the Leading with Heart program in 2018–2019. Their willingness to share their insights, their challenges and their stories as heart-led leaders was inspiring.

Contents

Praise for *Leading with Heart* . . . . *i*

Acknowledgements v

Foreword ix
Shelly L. Francis

Introduction:
Leading With Heart: Self-care, Collective Care, and Justice 1
Mary-Ann Mitchell-Pellett

Chapter 1 **Vulnerability as Self-Affirmation** 19
Debra Seaman

Chapter 2 **Heart Beats: Finding a Rhythm of Self-Care in Education** 33
Rob Chrol

Chapter 3 **Conflict and the Path To Wholeheartedly Embracing Leadership** 47
Jacqueline E.K Cameron

Chapter 4 **A Leader Emerges from a Manager** 59
Kimberley Dart

Chapter 5 **One Breath at a Time** 71
Lisa Talbot

Chapter 6 **The Sounds of Silence** 83
Katie McIntyre

Chapter 7 **Learning to be a Leader: Learning to Value Me** 95
Rachelle Savoie

Chapter 8 **Igniting ahcahk iskotew (spirit fire)** 107
Angela Sanregret

Chapter 9 **The Necessity of Self-Care for Professional Survival: Confessions of a New Leader** 121
Amelia Bird

Conclusion
Living With Heart: Self-care, Collective care, and Justice 133
Amy Burns

About the Authors: 141

About the Editors 143

Foreword

Shelly L. Francis

> Truth is an eternal conversation about things that matter, conducted with passion and discipline. Truth cannot possibly be found in the conclusions of the conversation, because the conclusions keep changing.
> —Parker J. Palmer, *Let Your Life Speak*

Welcome to an ongoing conversation about the importance of "leading with heart" and other things that matter, like justice, wellbeing, and trust. Many people have devoted their life's work to exploring these topics, offering their piece of the puzzle. The commitment to self-care and self-justice shown by the authors in these pages are evidence that a new generation of leaders is emerging to add their truth to this conversation.

These leaders are developing the capacity to lead from the heart, to embrace complexity with humility and creativity, because they have seen complexity in themselves and are brave enough to accept their shadows along with their light. They have experienced the power of community and recognize that social change will happen at the speed of trust. By learning to trust their own inner resources and each other, they know how to build trust across lines of difference. With those capacities in place, they are well-equipped to trust the unfolding complexities, uncertainties, and inequities in the world today. The good news is, with leaders like these authors, we are more likely to weather change with courage and a sense of being in it together.

When I began writing *The Courage Way*, a book for the Center for Courage & Renewal, I was daunted by the task of representing the wisdom of its founder, Parker J. Palmer, and the decades of work of countless facilitators in the US, Canada, Australia and beyond, who developed the practices known as the Circle of Trust® approach. I was daunted because at some level I was still wondering what we really meant by the word courage. The word comes from the French root *coeur*, or Latin *cor*, which means heart. I discovered that Thomas Aquinas wrote about bravery using the Latin word *fortitudo*, meaning strength. Fortitude is another word for courage. Combine them both and you get strength of heart. When we fortify ourselves, we gain courage. Fortify is also another word for self-care. Fortitude helps us take heart in places where it's so easy to lose heart, such as the world of education.

The Courage to Teach is a widely read, well-loved book Parker J. Palmer released in 1997 after decades of living his own questions about what that phrase means. I literally searched his books to find the word courage, seeking his answer. What I found instead was the word "encouragement."

In this new book you hold in your hands, notice how often the authors say that a teacher or mentor "encouraged me." A leader's job—and anyone who does this is leading—is to give encouragement to others, to help them recognize that they have more capacity than they realize. I'm glad that the authors explicitly name the word courage as a capacity one can recognize and develop. Here is a taste. Like a "found poem" (with only a bit of creative license), I gathered these phrases from the chapters ahead:

> *It takes courage to become a vulnerable, heart-led leader.*
>
> *It takes courage to muster the guts to speak your truth.*
>
> *It takes courage to reclaim and reassemble fragmented parts of your being that are separated through deforming societal patterns.*

It takes courage to share your feelings of overwhelm, perfectionism, and fear of owning your blind spots, to also embrace your light spots.

It takes courage to set down your lesson plan and practice "just being," to invite your students to join you.

It takes courage to set a table that invites others to show up with intention and respect.

It takes courage to step away from our preconceived ideas of leadership and embrace our human heart.

It takes courage to recognize negative self-talk and self-defeating actions, to speak from a place of awareness and authenticity instead.

It takes courage to speak up for what is right, even if it is uncomfortable.

It takes courage to know we can't engage in toxic conversations but can redirect the conversation or correct misinformation.

It takes courage to have difficult conversations, to persevere when work gets challenging and overwhelming.

It takes courage hold the space for people to talk about their thoughts and ideas, to help others feel heard and understood.

It takes courage to resolve or transform a situation for the better.

It takes courage to understand your own self with compassion and wisdom.

It takes courage to share something with another person, revealing what is important.

It takes courage to take a different path and start a new chapter in our collective story.

It takes courage to recognize that in order to support teachers or students, we must look after our own wellness.

I am heartened by the common vocabulary that has emerged over decades of ongoing conversation about the inner life of leaders, teachers, physicians, clergy, activists, not-for-profit and for-profit leaders, and people in all walks of life. I notice the frequency of naming and honoring concepts like "holding space," "presence," and "vulnerability." Mindfulness has become an accepted description of myriad beneficial practices that come from a lineage of wise teachers. My hope, and this book is proof it's possible, is for the word *wholeness* to become equally common, understood, cultivated, and valued.

I love hearing each author's first impressions about heart-led leadership, their willingness to share their personal story of growth from vulnerable doubts to empowered curiosity. The strong sense of voice and agency in these emerging leaders is palpable. (I believe the phrase "voice and agency" is code for courage.) It is a tribute to Dr. Mary-Ann Mitchell-Pellett's gifts as a teacher-leader that she was able to create a brave container for learning. That a cohort model was utilized for her students is not a small thing. The way she designed the learning experience includes some magic and mystery I'd like to point out, because shining a light on best-kept secrets may help the reader replicate results. This book is more than a description of what happened, but also shows how transformative education can nurture transformational leaders.

In each leader's story, you'll see five elements that blend to create courage in the classroom and in life, which I call the courage 'quintessentials.' Three key concepts are true self, trust, and community and two powerful practices are paradox and reflection. Heart-led leadership comes from knowing who you are at your core, including your values, your story, and even your shadows. Courage is not only in you, it is you, because in your moments of courage you meet your true self. Learning to trust your true self is a key to life and leadership, but we must also build trust between people we differ from and disagree with. And courage comes when we learn to trust in the unfolding of life overall. That's where community comes in. It takes courage to create community, and having a trustworthy community gives us a place to learn about ourselves and practice becoming a better human, so we have courage to go out into the world to "be the change we want to see."

The two key practices—paradox and reflection—are forms of mindfulness. Paradox helps us embrace complexity, not just between two true things that coexist, but between the multiple realities in today's world. We can learn to practice paradox by recognizing that the polarities that come with being human (life and death, love and loss, speaking and listening) are 'both-ands' rather than 'either-ors.' We can learn to let those tensions hold us in ways that stretch our hearts and minds open to new insights and possibilities.

The other key practice that cultivates courage is reflection, ideally within a community (or cohort) committed to discernment and growth, willing to hold deep conversations with compassion and curiosity, without shaming or judgment. In *Leading with Heart*, we see how this cohort of authors reflects on the value of true self, trust, community, and paradox. We see them grow in awareness, self-worth, and confidence.

Self-care is more than tending to one's body and mind, or avoiding work-related burnout. As these authors so aptly express, *care of true self* means to become aware of and spend time in one's own inner landscape. Only there can we reconnect to our meaning and purpose. Only there can we feel our way into wiser choices for ourselves and for the greater good. It's the inner landscape, full of bright colored tulips, fertile soil and unexpected weather, where seeds of new life might take hold and flourish. To prioritize self-care is an act of justice, both for self and those we care about. Leaders must give permission to others to make time for self-care. Heart-led leaders walk their talk by modeling self-care in action and leading system change to create cultures of wellness.

The soul of education as an institution is at a crisis point, like the other institutions on which society depends. The COVID-19 pandemic landed on top of countless refugees seeking asylum from war-torn countries, increasing suicide rates for teens, dropout rates for teachers, blatant racism, blind bias, vicious bullying, fractured politics, and the urgency of climate change. No problem has a quick fix or a single cause, but the trauma society is facing is mounting and triggering secondary trauma. Fear of the other, stress, burnout, and moral injury cannot be healed overnight. We can face it with fear, or we can face it with trust—together. The world is calling for a courage of all kinds—physical, moral, social, creative, and collective courage. We need our hearts along with heads and hands for the work ahead.

Given all that, I believe you'll feel hopeful after reading *Leading with Heart* because of all the good work being done to nurture the capacity for resilience, empathy, compassion, kindness, and self-aware living and leadership.

Educators are on the frontlines equipping and inspiring their learners to connect to their deepest truths and discover their greatest gifts. We need wholehearted leader-learners—like the one's you'll meet here—to remain in that role, because they will be the ones to nurture the next generation. In Rachael Kessler's 2000 book, *The Soul of Education*, she wrote:

> "Creating the climate and the skills for fostering creativity is essential to educating a generation of young people who can visualize new solutions to the problems of today and tomorrow's work force, social fabric, and environment. To these practical rationales for honoring the creative drive, I want to add the call from the soul. An 8th grade girl best captures this connection: 'Creativity is an outreach of your spirit into form,' she said. 'Then you can see it, hear, feel, touch it.'"

Each of these nine chapters, plus the "bookends" for context by Dr. Mary-Ann Mitchell-Pellett and Dr. Amy Burns, create a perspective of wholeness that you can see, hear, feel, and touch. Like describing an elephant for the first time from their own point of view, these voices create a vision of wellness, self-care, collective care, justice, and leadership we can all learn from. Sometimes we discover that the elephant in the room is ourselves, whose shadows we'd prefer to ignore. Sometimes the elephant in the room is multi-generational trauma and systemic injustice. By creating a community in which we can learn together, we will also discover the collective courage we need to move forward.

Enjoy and engage in this book's soulful conversation! I am quite grateful to have learned from the wholehearted leaders who've shared their stories within.

—Shelly L. Francis, author of
The Courage Way: Leading and Living with Integrity.

Introduction: Leading With Heart: Self-care, Collective Care, and Justice

Mary-Ann Mitchell-Pellett

Leading with heart is a popular theme found in many current approaches to leadership development programs. Within this topic are various perspectives of what *leading with heart* actually means. These perspectives include leading with love and compassion (Spaulding, 2015), finding meaningful work and service (Crowley, 2011), encouraging and empowering others (Kouzes & Posner, 2003), living and working with courage by being true to one's values and purpose (Tabrizi & Terrell, 2015), and understanding how emotions create quality connections and relationships (Crawford, 2009). Leading with heart also can also include developing the inner self and understanding how inner beingness outwardly manifests and impacts outer interactions with others and the organizations leaders serve – a symbiotic relationship between being (selfhood) and doing (action) (Fry & Kriger, 2009; Lips-Wiersma & Wright, 2012; Palmer, 2007).

The journey into leading with heart values both horizontal development (knowledge and skills) and vertical development (intrapersonal development and maturity) as necessary for effectively leading 21st-century environments. Leaders must skillfully lean into complexity and collaborate with diverse others in ways that involve a flexible and inclusive self-identity (Frizzel, Hoon, & Banner, 2016). Finding a balance within this awareness begins with an understanding that the leadership journey is not only about the leader. Brown (2019) reminds us that a leader is "anyone who takes responsibility for finding the potential in people and processes and has the courage to develop that potential" (p. 36). Hence, leadership invites an inward and outward focus.

This volume welcomes the above-mentioned ideas regarding leadership but goes beyond to explore how the inner journey of heart-led leadership is also connected to self-care, collective care, and justice, and embraces critical consciousness and action (Prilliltensky, 2011). It explores how emerging leaders can improve their ability to engage in collective care and the wellbeing of others by cultivating their own inner justice that begins with the practice of self-care.

Themes of wellness, self-care, and inspired leadership were popular topics within the realm of public education and leadership during a four-course graduate topic for Master of Education students, entitled *Leading with Heart*. Through face-to-face and online conversations, as well as written and visual assignments over a period of ten months, educators and emerging leaders from public and post-secondary institutions shared personal and professional experiences with physical, emotional, and mental stresses. Some of these stresses were instigated by heavy workloads, their own students' behavioral and mental health challenges, disheartening bureaucratic structures, and cultural expectations that overwork and exhaustion are something to be endured. Several educators identified that they and their colleagues often contemplate alternate career paths as their sense of disempowerment grows.

Finding ways to realize personal wellness and self-care within work as a teacher and leader should be viable, yet many new leaders feel conflicted and unsure of how to do this effectively. Prilliltensky and Fox (2007) identified that numerous people experience conflict when deciding how best to meet personal, relational, and collective needs, all of which are foundational to wellness. Prilliltensky and Fox (2007) also emphasized that successfully meeting these needs depends upon the amount of *justice* people experience in each of these domains.

Justice as identified by Miller (1999) is the fair and equitable distribution of power, resources, and burdens. Thus, a lack of justice within these realms aligns with a leader's sense of powerlessness and feelings of being under-resourced and over-burdened. In response, many educators and leaders within public education are taking justice into their own hands through walking away from unhealthy systems in order to guard their own wellbeing. For many, this type of action is a form of self-care. Self-care is recognized as an act of justice for oneself and others and weaves together the personal and the collective as Chew (2016) explains:

> Self-care is learning how to live our lives in a way that we are mindful of how we are, knowing ourselves in a way that is holistic – how are we mentally, physically, spiritually, in our relationships, in our emotions. It is the understanding that the personal and the political are together. The personal has to be mindful of the collective, and the collective has to be mindful of the individual. (n.p.)

Additionally, self-care is viewed as a means to reclaim and reassemble fragmented parts of one's being that are separated through deforming societal patterns: "A symbol of patriarchal societies the world over … is the separation of mind, heart and body; feeling disembodied, disconnected rather than whole. These forms of separation create stress for individuals, organizations and societies" (Wellbeing Advisory Group, 2016, n.p.). Therefore, for many teachers and leaders, it is important that they make a claim upon their wholeness, particularly as they experience the suffering of separation within themselves and within the hearts, minds, and bodies of their students. The interdependence between self-care, collective care, justice, and wellness, is close to the heart of educators and leaders and these connections will be discussed further in the upcoming sections.

Becoming a Tall Tulip: Intrapersonal Justice

As an instructor for a heart-led leadership development program, I notice that common conversations surface regarding the practice of self-care. While sitting in our newly formed cohorts of education students who aspire to leadership, many discussed their need for self-care and the difficulty of maintaining the practice of it. These students also shared concerns that other people in their work or personal circles often consider the journey of inner exploration and self-care as "belly button gazing" and an outward form of selfishness. However, after more discussion, there arose a general consensus that self-care is necessary, as long as it doesn't go "too far" and result in one's head getting stuck in their belly button. Students suggested that they need to be on guard lest the practice of self-care turn one into a "tall tulip" type of human who thinks they are somehow more advanced than everyone else. Those tall tulip types, they said, will get "smacked down."

However, as the discussion of the tall tulip metaphor advanced, students began questioning why a tall tulip needs to be cut down. Why can't a person be tall tulip if that is who they are? Why does a person have to play *small* in order to make others feel better about themselves? What if being a tall tulip is a person's birthright and arises from the practice of taking one's rightful place in the world? Students entertained the possibility that becoming a tall tulip means that a person is embracing their potential and has found the courage to let it become a resource, which is very different than "showing off." Thus, the metaphor of the tall tulip that arose in one of our program groups became a powerful and significant symbol of the strength and integrity of the self, as well as the self-justice that arises from courageous action when standing against those things in our culture that want to cut us down.

Connections between justice, self-care, and wellbeing is supported by Prilliltensky (2011) who suggests that justice and wellbeing naturally inform and impact one another. He identified that research in organizational development correlates a lack of justice in the workplace to physical illness, psychological issues, and problems with job satisfaction and performance. Within his ecological model of justice and wellbeing, Prilliltensky (2011) suggests that difficulties at the personal, interpersonal, organizational, and communal levels when wellness is not present are caused by lower levels of justice operating in those environments. Conversely, higher levels of justice equate with higher levels of wellbeing. Therefore, it is particularly important to support empowerment, control, and responsibility for one's own wellbeing, so that on the personal level people act with justice towards themselves (Prilliltensky, 2011).

In our leadership development circles, students shared stories about the various forms of "psychological injustices" (Prilliltensky, 2011, n.p.) they endure, such as self-depreciating thoughts and behaviors, or feelings of unworthiness, which inevitably leads to unnecessary suffering for the self and others. Almost every student identified that they have felt diminished or oppressed by others' leadership. As Palmer (1999) explains, "A leader shapes the ethos in which others must live, an ethos as light-filled as heaven or as shadowy as hell" (p. 79). Furthermore, the students became aware that their own leadership has the capacity to be "shadowy" if they lack the awareness and understanding about their own patterns and reaction within their interactions. Thus, an important question arises: *How can teachers and educational leaders effectively become self-aware and sustainable, while contributing to the healthy sustainability of their schools, their students, and public education?*

As emerging leaders explore possible answers to the above-mentioned question, they become aware of the importance of bringing one's whole self to the work as a leader, with the understanding that "everything a person does is part of an integrated whole and creates a net effect in happiness or suffering" (Bunting, 2016, p. 24). Thus, heart-led leadership development should teach students practices and habits of the heart (Palmer, 2011), which can facilitate an inward awareness and explorations that lead to deeper personal and professional wholeness. For example, students often report that the inward journey provides insight into important values, dreams, and desires of the heart, as well as the opportunity to define a personal vision guided by clarity and authenticity. Students begin to realize that "there is no difference between becoming an effective leader and becoming a fully integrated human being" (Brendel & Bennett, 2016, p. 410).

Qualities that arise from attuning to the heart, such as compassion and loving-kindness for the self and others is also important. Through mindful heart-centering practices, students report an increased ability to accept themselves, their colleagues, and their students with compassionate understanding. Self-compassion engenders courage, acceptance, and a will to change when exploring "shadow" aspects of self that need improvement. Accepting that the goal is not perfection helped students to embrace their humanity with compassion and learn from both their experiences and from helpful feedback.

Strength and resilience were also common themes of the inner journey in leadership formation. Many students reported that they became less critical of the self, gaining a better understanding that leaders need to embrace the path of the lifelong learner. Through the study of Hanson's (2018) work on resilience, students engaged in practices such as "taking in the good" (p. 57) that helped them feel more resourced and connected – both internally and externally to the positive things in their lives. They also learned how to be with both their own and others' uncomfortable emotions, thoughts, and processes in more effective ways. Students also develop fortitude or inner strength and learn how to "hold their seat" – a term borrowed from equestrian dressage, in which a person learns how to sit firmly in the saddle, through absorbing movement without applying tension. In essence, emerging leaders can learn how to hang on through difficult times with dignity and with more ease.

It is crucial that emerging leaders become more aware of their impact during their interactions with others. Leaders who lead from a center of wellness and nonreactivity create a space where others are more apt to feel these ways too (Bunting, 2016). *Being* affects *doing* – what is inside of us flows outward to help form or inform ourselves, others, and the world in a constant exchange of the inner and outer (Center for Courage & Renewal, & Francis, 2018). When awareness and responsibility for this exchange takes place on a personal level, intrapersonal justice for the self is deepened, as well as the ability to engage with others in a way that can facilitate interpersonal justice.

Growing Fields of Tulips: Interpersonal Justice

Relational and interpersonal justice is about treating others with dignity and respect, and not harming others through superior physical, psychological, or economic resources (Prilliltensky, 2011). Justice is also about balancing what is due to the self, with what is due to other people, institutions and communities (Sheppard, Lewicki, & Minton, 1992). Emerging leaders can learn to support others in becoming tall tulips and in finding the will and courage to help correct the things that shade others' share of the sun. It is not easy to change oppressive structures that allow only tall tulips to rise from the soil of privilege. Supporting others to become tall tulips is an important part of preserving others' dignity that leads to wellbeing, as Prilliltensky (2011) advocates: "Justice is also not just about what is given but also about how it is given. Human beings are extremely protective of their dignity; it is soul food. This is why processes of justice and subjective elements of wellbeing are so crucial. Wounds to the soul may be as harmful as wounds to the body" (n.p.).

Thus, the act of self-care (intrapersonal wellness) extends outwards towards others and helps support webs of interpersonal wellness. Self-care that is integrated into the broader cultures of community care can help to sustain more people in relationship to one another (Michaeli, 2017). Students in our leadership development classes share their dreams and desire to work in "flourishing systems where people are encouraged and empowered to be well" (Prilliltensky, 2011, p. 13). They wonder how they can work collectively to help close the gap between nonflourishing and flourishing schools, systems, and communities. For many, it is apparent that they need to develop and mature their own inner resources, to find effective anchors that can sustain them on their leadership journey, as they serve the greater good of their communities. Many of these inner resources, such as goodness, responsiveness, and clarity arise from what Bunting (2016) calls "heartfulness," and the practice of mindfulness is considered one of the primary tools for this type of development.

Mindfulness as a leadership development tool is an effective way to deepen self-understanding and transformation, not only for its own sake, but to help reduce suffering for others. Magee (2016) reiterates that mindfulness practice facilitates both intrapersonal growth (learning from our own experiences with social suffering) and interpersonal growth (effectively offering support across lines of diversity), helping leaders work alongside others to relieve suffering at all levels and make lasting changes. As an instructor in a heart-led leadership development program where mindfulness practices are used, I hear students share transformative stories and examples throughout the year that portray how these practices are a cornerstone tool in helping them become justice-oriented, heart-led leaders for the self and others.

The Inspired Leadership Map

In learning how to bridge understanding and effective leadership from self to others, emerging leaders in our heart-led leadership program found support and guidance through an "Inspired Leadership" map (Mitchell-Pellett, 2020; see Figure 1) that followed students throughout a four-course program on leading with heart. Students created insightful leadership maps using visual documentation and expression of their leadership development over a ten-month period. These visual archives can articulate the interconnected facets of their journey, as well as how these aspects were responsible for developing and transforming aspects of the self in order to positively effect self-care, community care, and justice.

Inspired Leadership arises from the *personal wellness* of the body, mind, emotions, and heart. Wellness for leaders is particularly important due to their influence, as reiterated by Thich Nhat Hanh: "When we are well, our wellness spills onto others; When we are unwell that too spills over onto others. Be well" (Bunting, 2016, p. 20). "Wellness is the conscious development of the whole self" (Global Wellness Day, 2020). By cultivating development of the whole person, a leader invigorates and *breathes life* into the self and others. The word inspire, is taken from the Latin *inspirare*, "to breathe or blow into," (Merriam-Webster, n.d.). Thus, inspired leadership contains the seeds of wellness, whereby one is connected to the self and all beings in healthy, life-giving ways.

Inspired Leadership is *self-leadership*. Leading others effectively comes from being able to cultivate and lead one's best self through self-awareness, self-management, knowing one's heart, values, and vision, and bringing purposeful meaning to action. Self-leadership is a lifelong process: "No leader sets out to become a leader. People set out to live their lives, expressing themselves fully. When that expression is of value, they become leaders. The point is to become yourself.... You must withhold nothing. You must in sum, become the person you started out to be, and to enjoy the process of becoming," (Bennis, 2003).

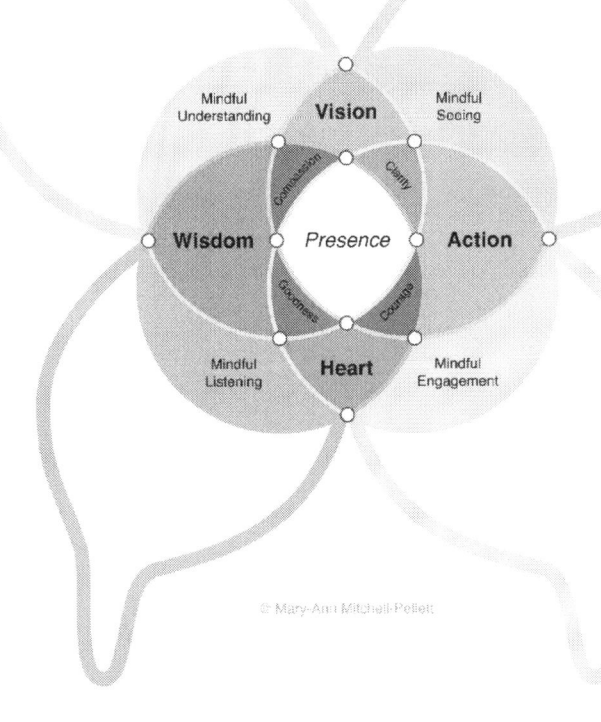

Inspired Leadership

Diagram showing four overlapping circles labeled Vision, Action, Heart, and Wisdom, intersecting at Presence. Outer labels: Mindful Understanding, Mindful Seeing, Mindful Engagement, Mindful Listening. Inner connectors: Compassion, Clarity, Courage, Openness. © Mary-Ann Mitchell-Pellett

Inspired Leadership includes the practice of *mindfulness,* which has many benefits for leaders, such as increased resilience, improved emotional intelligence, an ability to build trusting relationships, and physical, emotional, and mental wellness. Mindfulness deepens self-exploration and self-acceptance (Bunting, 2016), and creates a presence that others perceive as trustworthy and benevolent. Mindfulness also brings awareness to the quality of one's *being while doing* (Lyddy & Good, 2017) enabling a leader to consider: *Right now, in this moment, am I being open or critical? Kind or unkind? Defensive or inquiring?* Mindfulness helps leaders manage their inner worlds, as they respond to the complexities of the outer world in healthy ways.

When freedom, growth, and creativity are cultivated in the human self, inspiration is unleashed (Bunting, 2016). The metaphor of the journey of the caterpillar into a butterfly is representative of this process. However, it is not easy work, as reiterated by Bennis (2009), who suggests that leaders are made through hard work. The success of a leader is supported through one's level of self-development, which is a lifelong process. Bunting (2016) proposes that personal development be taken as far as it can, as the point is not to become a caterpillar with wings, which would not be very effective – but to become the whole and beautifully developed butterfly!

The Inspired Leadership map explores the benefits of connecting to *heart, wisdom, vision*, and *action* - resources found in other leadership development models (Arrien, 1993; Kouzes & Posner, 2003). *mindful listening, mindful understanding, mindful seeing,* and *mindful engagement* are process tools that deepen the understanding and application of these resources for inspired leadership. Additionally, mindfulness practices help develop awareness of human *goodness, compassion*, *clarity*, and *courage*, which adds greater resiliency. The intersecting points of the map elements (or "sweet spots") are opportunities for further contemplation related to how these elements work together to bring about positive growth. The major sweet spot of *presence* at the center of the map informs leaders of how *compassionate awareness* holds the whole process together.

Heart

Connecting to the heart is where true inspiration arises from the foundation of care. Becoming aware of what one cares about is important and includes asking *Who am I? What do I love or care deeply about? What do I value? What is my spark? Why am I here?* Additionally, practices geared to raising awareness of the heart connect leaders to self-compassion, self-care, and self-justice. Personal exploration related to identity and wellness, can also bring up issues related to shame and feelings of being flawed (Brown, 2018). Cultivating self-care and self-compassion provides the needed balm to relieve the suffering in one's mind and heart. Additionally, the heart provides the strength to help leaders show up with their gifts and abilities and brings justice to their purpose as human beings and in leading others.

Learning *how* to listen to the heart and one's inner self brings awareness to the seeds of identity and one's birthright gifts: "Before I can tell my life what I want to do with it, I must listen to my life telling me who I am" (Palmer, 1999). We begin with cultivating awareness of the sensations of the body and breath, and turn to noticing beliefs, thoughts, feelings, and patterns. With compassion and nonjudgement, we listen to the content of thoughts and the patterns of our lives as these show up in the body and mind. We listen again and again to the yearning of our hearts. We also learn how to mindfully listen to others and provide a space for them to listen to their own hearts instead of trying to fix or save them. We learn to create a space within the body, mind, and heart where the *inner teacher* can be heard (Palmer, 1998).

Goodness: "I am Worthy"

Mindful listening to the body and heart reveals the truth of one's inner *goodness* and wholeness. Goodness is the best part of one's self, and we realize that there is more right with us than we think (Kabat-Zinn, 2012). We realize that thoughts of unworthiness are just thoughts – not reality. Mindfulness practices helps put our beliefs, thoughts, and emotions in a bigger container of reality, providing space for healthier views of the self to emerge. This *view* of the self is foundational to the work of leaders: *How we see ourselves is how we will see others.* As we see and feel the natural dignity (Kornfield, 2008) we are born with, we engage in self-justice by taking a stand to uphold this dignity, our inner wisdom, and in our *right* to be leaders in a variety of ways, particularly leading the best of ourselves into the world. As Walt Whitman (2009) reiterates, "I am larger and better than I thought. I did not think I held so much goodness."

Wisdom

Wisdom arises when the heart is open and receptive (Kornfield, 2008). It also takes wisdom to know where one is competent or needs humility for learning. Leaders need *practical wisdom* to respond to everyday issues and *conceptual wisdom* to integrate an understanding of self and the existential issues of life (Walsch, 2015). Developing the ability to cultivate wisdom from a variety of sources is invaluable, as new perspectives re-inform previously held wisdom and deepens understanding. There is also a correlation between wisdom, compassion, and benevolence, and Walsch (2015) advocates that the wiser one is, the greater the number of beings he will seek to benefit, "in fact wisdom is nothing but knowing the way of benevolence," (Sung-hae, cited in Walsch, 2015, p. 18).

Mindful Understanding

Mindful listening and mindful understanding are like two wings of a bird. Mindful listening cultivates better understanding of the self, others, and important issues. Mindfully listening to the inner wisdom of the self, as well as the experience and wisdom of others' perspectives, develops deeper understandings. For example, through mindful listening, one learns how to listen to the body, which is an important source of information and embodied wisdom. By listening to the body, one can locate the wisdom of the head, heart, and gut and connect these parts for greater understanding, taking the time that wisdom needs for development. (Oelke & deVos, 2020). So, we slow down, listen, and allow mindful understandings to grow into deeper insights. We also use the process of mindful inquiry and reflection to check our thoughts, attitudes, and stories, which helps us to better understand our motives, intentions, and actions.

Compassion "I Care/I Love"

Self-compassion helps people honor their goodness and become shame-resilient, since people who believe they are worthy of connection and belonging are more likely to reach out for support and experience empathy from others (Brown, 2018). Self-compassion prepares the way for exploring and changing unhealthy beliefs, thoughts, and patterns, and one becomes a light for the self (Brach, 2019). Additionally, holding others' stories with compassion and nonjudgement supports understanding about what they need and helps to teach others how they could hold their own selves in a more caring way. It is a great gift to help others return to the awareness of their own goodness (Salzberg, 2004).

Vision

Having a personal vision awakens the best in us by reconnecting us to what is important, such as our values (Bunting, 2016). Having a personal vision is necessary, as leaders must seek out and align themselves with causes and organizations that match their values. Having a vision provides intentionality, engagement, and presence, and it must also be benevolent and worth pursuing (Walsch, 2015). A benevolent vision arises from the intersection of heart and wisdom, for it is only through an aware heart that a leader sees clearly the needs of others or has the compassionate motivation to enhance others' wellbeing beyond the self. When vision is informed by heart and wisdom, it is selfless and much more powerful than an agenda based on ego, as it receives energy and passion from the heart to move the vision forward.

Mindful Seeing and Clarity: "I See What is Worthy"

Mindful seeing involves the process of observing things just as they are. An important practice is that of *not knowing* and letting go of fixed opinions about self, others, and situations. Fleet Maull (2019) calls it the *not-knowing mind*, or nonconceptual mind, where one steps out of the conditioned mind to directly and openly experience and see things as they are. When one is willing to experience and witness something without the protection of *knowing* in advance, insight and wisdom will arise on its own. When we don't know what to do, we can listen, and practice not knowing, trusting that insight will come.

Action

Action that is based on the wisdom and vision of the heart reduces suffering and brings wellness and justice for others and the self. Wise action is the work of heart-led leaders. Additionally, as we grow in self-leadership, we naturally support others' leadership development, knowing we all benefit when everyone is able to show up with their voices, gifts, and contributions. There is no room for envy when strong self-leadership is practiced because we understand and reap the benefits when everyone shows up with their gifts and unique medicine for the world. We value diversity in a diverse world. When the actions of leaders are infused with heart, wisdom, and vision, those leaders are most likely to be engaged, healthy, and well.

Mindful Engagement

Mindfulness-based practices can support leaders in approaching their day-to-day experiences mindfully. Mindfulness is considered a *state of being* where people are actively aware of themselves and their surroundings, and process their experience from multiple perspectives: "mindful engagement is about how leaders can approach their experiences, go through their experiences, and reflect on their experiences in ways that enhance the lessons of experience," (Ashford & DeRue, 2012, p. 146). Mindful engagement is also fostered through the compassion we feel when we are touched by the suffering of others, thus compelling us to step into action and do something about it, from a response based on heart and wisdom.

Courage: "I Show Up"

It takes courage to lead with the integrity of one's heart and values. Self-leadership provides clarity about who one is, and what is important. When one is infused with the "strength of the heart," which is the real meaning of courage (Center for Courage & Renewal & Francis, 2018), one finds strength and fortitude. With courage, one shows up, and can stay when things heat up. With courage one is open to the world and open to life without armoring – while there is a "yes" in compassion, there is also a "no" in the courageous heart (Kornfield, 2020). A courageous heart is willing to stand up and say "no" to abuse, violence, and those things that violate the heart. Courage is required to help carry out wise action.

Presence

The center or major sweet spot is *presence*, where all elements of the map intersect and are held together with awareness. "Presence is a space of heartfulness, wholeness, and wakefulness, that we experience in each moment ... and with presence, one recognizes the interconnectedness of all things," (Kabat-Zinn, 2019, n.p.). As well, presence is *embodied*, which means we are aware of the present moment though our bodies and senses and are having a conversation with our direct experience: "We need to be fully alive in our bodies and we need presence for empathy, wonder, and connection. To be present means we are light unto ourselves, as we explore our human experiences in the present moment, we are illuminated and become wiser" (Brach, 2019, n.p.).

Community of Care

In working with students of leadership development, the formation of a community of care is crucial to supporting this kind of inner work and growth. The personal will to risk and grow can be encouraged through actions that create non-judgemental, caring, and safe practices. As an instructor for our leadership development program, I used elements and practices of the Circles of Trust© processes inspired by the Center for Courage & Renewal (2019), from my training as a facilitator of this approach. The authentic community that was built through and around the work students completed throughout the year was one of the highlights of building a cohort model that is longer-term and dedicated to leadership development. Students found a community of safety and trust, where they explored their own roles related to the suffering of self and others, and ways to reduce this suffering. These communities extend beyond the completion of the program in a variety of ways, and the emerging writers of these upcoming chapters discuss the importance of this. Doing the inner and outer work required for heart-led leadership includes efforts from both individuals and a caring community. Thus, all "tall tulips" can grow and inspire others with their inherent beauty and loveliness.

References

Angeles, A., (1993). *The four-fold way: Walking the paths of the warrior, teacher, healer, and visionary.* New York, NY: HarperOne.

Ashford, S. J., & DeRue, D. S. (2017). Developing as a leader: The power of mindful engagement. *Organizational Dynamics, 41,* 146–154. https:doi.org/10.1016/j.orgdyn.2012.01.008

Bennis, D. (2003). *On becoming a leader: A leadership classic.* New York, NY: Basic Books.

Brach, T. (2019). *Embodied presence: Portal to the sacred part 1* [video file]. Retrieved from https://www.youtube.com/watch?v=BeCXBpRfNl0

Brendel, W., & Bennett, C. (2016). Learning to embody leadership through mindfulness and somatics practice. *Advances in Developing Human Resources, 18*(3), 409–425.

Brown, B. (2019). *Dare to lead: Brave work, tough conversations, whole hearts.* New York, NY: Random House.

Bunting, M. (2016). *The mindful leader: 7 practices for transforming your leadership, your organisation and your life.* Melbourne, Australia: John Wiley & Sons.

Center for Courage & Renewal & Francis, S. L. (2018). *The courage way: Leading and living with integrity.* Oakland, CA: Berrett-Koehler.

Chew, L. (2016). Self-care and collective wellbeing, [Webinar summary, November 3, 2016] Retrieved from https://www.awid.org/news-and-analysis/webinar-summary-self-care-and-collective-wellbeing

Crawford, M. (2009). *Getting to the heart of leadership: Emotion and educational leadership.* London: Sage Publications.

Crowley, M. C. (2015). *Lead from the heart: Transformational leadership for the 21st century.* Bloomington, IN: Balboa Press.

Frizzell, D. A., Hoon, S., & Banner, D. K. (2016). A phenomenological investigation of leader development and mindfulness meditation. *Journal of Social Change, 8*(1), 14–25.

Fry, L., & Kriger, M. (2009). Towards a theory of being-centered leadership: Multiple levels of being as context for effective leadership. *Human Relations, 62*(1), 1667–1696.

Global Wellness Day, (2020). What is wellness? [Online]. Retrieved from http://www.globalwellnessday.org/about/what-is-wellness/

Hanson, R. (2018). *Resilient: How to grow an unshakable core of calm, strength, and happiness.* New York, NY: Harmony Books.

Merriam-Webster (n.d.). Inspire [definition]. Retrieved on January 1, 2020, from https://www.merriam-webster.com/dictionary/inspire

Kabat-Zinn, J. (1994). *Wherever you go, there you are: Mindfulness meditation in everyday life*. New York, NY: Hyperion.

Kabat-Zinn, J. (2019). *Cultivating embodied presence with Jon Kabat-Zinn*. [video file]. Sounds True. Retrieved from https://www.youtube.com/watch?v=iGJLNNYUXYk

Kouzes, J. M. & Posner, B. Z. (2003). *Encouraging the heart: A leader's guide to rewarding and recognizing others*. San Francisco, CA: Jossey-Bass.

Kornfield, J. (2008). *The wise heart: A guide to the universal teachings of Buddhist psychology*. New York, NY: Random House.

Kornfield, J. (2020). The courageous heart [Online]. Retrieved from https://jack-kornfield.com/the-courageous-heart/

Lips-Wiersma, M., & Wright, S. (2012). Measuring the meaning of meaningful work: Development and validation of the comprehensive meaningful work scale (CMWS). *Group & Organization Management, 37*(5), 655–685.

Lyddy, C. J. & Good, D. J. (2017). Being while doing: An inductive model of mindfulness at work. Frontiers of Psychology, 7(2060). https://doi.org/10.3389/fpsyg.2016.02060

Magee, R. (2019). *The inner work of racial justice: Healing ourselves and transforming communities through mindfulness*. New York, NY: TarcherPerigree.

Maull, F. (2019). *How to move beyond blame, fearlessly live your highest purpose, and become an unstoppable force for good*. Bounder, CO: Sounds True.

Michaeli, I. (2017). Self-care: An act of political warfare or a neoliberal trap? *Development, 60*, 50–56.

Miller, D. (999) *Principles of social justice*. Cambridge, MA: Harvard University Press.

Mitchell-Pellett, M. (2020). *Inspired Leadership map*. Calgary, AB.

Oelke, R., & deVos, C. (Producers). (2020, February 10). Inhabit: Your wisdom [audio podcast]. Retrieved from https://integrallife.com/inhabit-your-wisdom/

Palmer, P. (1998). *The courage to teach: Exploring the inner landscape of a teacher's life*. San Francisco, CA: Jossey-Bass.

Palmer, P. (1999). *Let your life speak*. San Francisco, CA: Jossey-Bass.

Palmer, P. (2007). *The hidden wholeness: A journey toward an undivided life*. San Francisco, CA: Jossey-Bass.

Palmer, P. (2011). *Five habits of the heart*. Retrieved from http://www.couragerenewal.org/habitsoftheheart/

Prilliltensky, I., & Fox, D. R. (2007). Psychopolitical literacy for wellness and justice. *Journal of Community Psychology*, *35*(6), 793–805. https://doi.org/10.1002/jcop.20179

Prilliltensky, I. (2011). Wellness as fairness. *American Journal of Community Psychology*, *49*(1–2), 1–21. https://doi.org/10.1007/s10464-011-9448-8

Salzberg, S. (2004). *Lovingkindness: The revolutionary art of happiness*. Boulder, CO: Shambala Publications.

Spaulding, T. (2015). *The heart-led leader: How living and leading from the heart will change your organization and your life*. New York, NY: Crown.

Sheppard, B., Lewicki, R., & Minton, J. (1992). *Organizational justice: The search for fairness in the workplace*. New York: Maxwell Macmillan.

Tabrizi, B., & Terrell, M. (2015). *The inside out effect: A practical guide to transformational leadership*. Ashland, OH: Evolve Publishing.

Walsch, R. (2015). What is wisdom? Cross-cultural and cross-disciplinary synthesis. *Review of General Psychology*. *19*(3), 278–293. https://doi.org/10.1037/gpr0000045

Wellbeing Advisory Group, (2016). Concept Paper: Wellbeing [Google doc]. Retrieved on March 15, 2020, from http://bit.ly/2hSkmwu

Whitman, W. (2009). *Leaves of grass: The original 1855 edition*. American Renaissance Books.

Chapter 1

Vulnerability as Self-Affirmation

Debra Seaman

"No one belongs here more than you"
(Brown, 2017, p.158).

Vulnerability. It's a word that is hard to explain. It's a state of being that can be difficult to honor and accept in oneself. It certainly isn't something I would have ever knowingly welcomed, although I've encountered it more times than I'd like to admit. Vulnerability involves, "uncertainty, risk, and emotional exposure" (Brown, 2018, p. 34). When I am vulnerable, I take a risk to show others who I am, authentically, without caving into fear about the responses and judgements of others, although the fear lingers. Like many people, being the opposite of vulnerable is more my style. Closed. Silent. Strong. What Brown (2012) refers to as vulnerability armor. However, an armored approach creates a false sense of safety, along with a false image about who I am. Vulnerability is also linked to wholeheartedness, a necessary component of wholehearted leadership that helps to foster authenticity, self-compassion, resiliency, and even play and rest (Brown, 2012), and is essential to inspired leadership.

Without consciously knowing it, I have worked towards being a wholehearted leader. During the past four years, I have been a learning leader in two different schools, with roles including that of instructional coach, literacy and task design specialist, as well as a team leader for grade-level teams. Learning leaders are mid-level leaders who are appointed by their principals, and they play an important role in advancing school innovation and student learning (Brown, Friesen, & Marcotte, 2017). The role of learning leader is also an important stepping-stone for assistant principal and principal positions in many school districts. I embarked upon a master's degree in order to further support my leadership development, but my journey with vulnerability was certainly not the path I had intended to follow. However, I am so thankful that I did open the door to vulnerability, as it helped me grow as an authentic leader. The purpose of this chapter is to share my process and struggles with vulnerability—a vulnerable act itself—with the hope that others who wear that vulnerability armour can see the benefits of being vulnerable in developing leadership. Vulnerability has become my strength. It has helped develop who I am as a leader by providing me with more confidence in my abilities and the potential to grow. It has also impacted the way I work with others as a learning leader.

Taking the First Vulnerable Step

Place yourself into my shoes for a moment. As a learning leader and educator who is always on the go, and who also struggles to take time for herself, you can imagine my reaction when I entered the first day of class of a leadership program geared towards developing *the heart* of the leader. Chairs formed a circle, providing a face-to-face view of everyone, with no desks to hide behind. Mindfulness practices abounded, left, right, and center. We were encouraged to explore feelings, thoughts, hopes, and dreams, along with our shadows and fears. I questioned if this was the right program for me. *Was it too late to change to something normal? If all of this was happening on the first day of the class, how deep would we be going by week two? Would I even last?* I was anxious before we even started.

The previous year, I had taken a very logical instructional leadership program, and I intended to follow up with a course on active learning environments. Solid, linear topics that didn't leave me feeling uncertain and confused. Courses that could help this learning leader land a job as a future school principal. However, vulnerability obviously had other plans for me, as colleagues and peers convinced me to try me a leadership program that explored the resources of the heart. I ended up biting the bullet and signed up with as open a mind as I could manage.

Taking that first step to sit in the circle with a group of strangers, vulnerability and all, was difficult. Although the instructor always provided an invitation to share, a part of me held back. There was no way I was ready to share *anything* with a room full of strangers. Yet there was also a part of me that longed to let myself be known—if even in a small way. Connection is why we are here (Brown, 2010), and this wisdom has always informed my work as an educator and learning leader. I longed to connect, to be seen and heard, and yet every part of my being was afraid. Something inside me, that courage we all have deep down, pushed me past the fear. I started small by asking others questions; more in-depth sharing would take time, however. Initially I didn't see this circle as an invitation to learn, grow, and listen to new ideas. Instead, I armored up in my usual way, and decided to protect myself; to fake it in an effort to fit in, while holding back my real self.

I noticed this experience was similar to my first administration team meeting as a new learning leader. Again, there I was, the new one in the circle with my principal, assistant principal, and other learning leaders who had mentored me. I was afraid to speak, afraid to share, afraid to screw up, especially being new to the role. However, in spite of this fear, something stronger and courageous arose. I knew I was there for a reason. I knew I was there to help make changes for the better, and that I wouldn't be sitting in that meeting if others didn't see the value I was bringing to the table in the first place. How could I not speak, knowing that was exactly why I was there? In both situations I listened until I couldn't listen anymore, and finally I spoke up. Everything turned out all right that time, and so I decided to open my mind and heart and give this new group a chance. At this point, I think I gave myself a small affirmation, which was greatly needed, and reminded myself that I had something to offer as a leader and that I did belong.

One step at a time, vulnerability opened my heart, and my fixed mind began to slowly crack. Once during a break, a fellow classmate commented on how something I said had caused her to rethink her position and take a pause. I didn't even remember what I said. For a short second, I thought, *Ok, maybe I can do this. Maybe I do belong.* Knowing someone else had found value in what I said helped me to understand that maybe I had something to offer others by sharing what was important to me, what was part of my heart. I found a new confidence in taking a risk to share my voice. This was a key insight that helped me move forward: I could hold a space for my fear and vulnerability while sharing my strengths and wisdom to a group at the same time. "Vulnerability is the core, the heart … of meaningful human experiences" (Brown, 2012, p. 12). *How was I to grow as a leader and help create meaningful experiences for others without being vulnerable?*

Sitting in the circle and listening to my classmates share their stories was eye-opening. People were sharing their personal experiences related to becoming a leader, which included admitting they didn't know it all. They were modeling vulnerability, and they asked questions in the hopes that we could dip into some of our own experiences and wisdom to help or advise them. As our circle began to feel safe, I realized I was hiding from a group of people whom I knew had already accepted me. What was I really hiding from I wondered? If there was an opportunity to learn how to become more vulnerable, in a safe space, something told me this was it. By this time, I had started to notice patterns in my rumblings with vulnerability. I recalled a previous administrative meeting when my all-knowing principal, (as I defined her), asked us questions and had asked for our help. She was a model of vulnerability. She was open, willing to ask for support, and she listened intently to the suggestions we brought forward. Her leadership was inspiring, and kept coming to mind as what vulnerability could look like in practice as a leader. It started to come together for me. I did not always have to be *the strongest, most knowledgeable* person in a room. Asking for support was important and necessary, and reminded me to not be so hard on myself. How could I possibly know everything about everything? How could anyone?

One Step Forward, One Step Back, Two Steps Forward

Slowly I became more comfortable in our circle and I began to show my newly emerging vulnerable side. That is, until the crying began. I dread crying in front of others or witnessing others crying in public. Additionally, gestures of empathy from others when I cry feels like *pity* to me. So, imagine my terror when a classmate cried. This wasn't a single, gentle tear rolling out of the corner of an eye, but the full-on waterworks. Aware of my discomfort, I searched for my water bottle and wondered how I could leave the room inconspicuously while sitting in a circle. I prayed for my invisibility powers to kick in, not fully realizing that I was really hiding from my own feelings of discomfort. The other members in the group looked quite fine with this display of emotions, and I didn't see anyone else running for the door. However, all I could think was: *How can someone be this vulnerable in front of strangers? And why would they want to be?* I honestly did not get it. Clearly, a minor setback in my new journey into vulnerability, and thirty-six years of armoring was not going to be broken in two days.

Although vulnerability can feel terrifying, excruciating even (Brown, 2012), I also realized that I had a lot of company. Like many, I was afraid of being viewed in a negative light: I was "prone to worry about negative evaluations, rejection, alienating the other person, losing self-esteem and control over the situation" (Bruk, Scholl, & Bless, 2018, p. 193). Opening up to other people conjures images of weakness, incompetence, and failures. These are not traits people want in a leader, but we often see them because of leaders' unwillingness to be vulnerable. I remember a team meeting when a former assistant principal said, "I don't know the answer to that right now." What an amazing experience. I actually admired this response, and my administrator even more, as she reflected how vulnerability creates connection and trust. I knew my administrator wasn't going to make up stuff on the spot because she didn't know something—something we have likely all experienced, and also likely have noted it as being very inauthentic and alienating to others. Witnessing a leader's ability to be vulnerable helped me get a bit closer to being willing to practice more of it myself, as I could clearly fathom its benefits.

Learning to become a vulnerable leader has involved reflecting and inquiring into my own thoughts, feelings, and actions. I'd never explored myself as fully as I did when learning to become a heart-led leader. In the beginning, I was making every effort to focus on how this type of learning just applied to my professional life as an educator. However, I realized that I was trying to hide the personal, emotional, and messy parts, and these parts were essential to how I would show up as a leader.

As though on a Mobius strip journey (Parker, 2004), I was forced to see how the traits I perceived to be negative about myself (written on one side of the paper) connected, informed, and resonated with my positive traits (written on the opposite side of the paper). In fact, this wasn't just a mental exercise, a metaphorical journey; I took pen to paper and created a visual aid. While twisting this little, insignificant piece of paper into a Mobius strip, I was forced to see their interconnections and how difficult it was to separate them. I gained insight into the fact that my perceived negative traits were actually my own potential, ready to learn, grow, and become more useful. I also started to understand that self-transformation and change has been taking place in my own life over the years, whether I wanted to admit it or not.

In fact, I related this exercise back to a time when I was a child. Growing up, I was afraid of everything, and I was so shy it was painful. I remember going to SeaWorld and being afraid to get splashed by the whales, so I made my Mom sit out of the splash zone with me. I was afraid to go on rides when we visited Canada's Wonderland. I used to dread talking to new people; I would actually hide behind my mother when people came to talk to us. Then one day, all this changed. My father says it was a *position of power* that changed me. I became assistant stage manager for a school play, which allowed me to boss everyone else around. Inadvertently, I learned how to connect with a new sense of personal power and courage. I don't know if it was this particular position or something else that made me more confident, but I suddenly became a chatterbox who liked new adventures, travel, and talking to total strangers. I became a person who wanted to be in the spotlight and relished public speaking.

However, along with transforming my shy self into someone with greater confidence, I also swung to the other side: I learned somewhere that being strong was affiliated with *not* asking others for help. This, I believe, is where the armoring patterns begin for many of us, often very early in life. Somewhere along the way I got the idea that the qualities of strong and vulnerable were to be only found on the opposite ends of that Mobius strip, never to touch. I also thought I could only show the *strong* side, not realizing that on a Mobius strip, the vulnerable side actually intersects with the strong side. Whether I like it or not these two sides of the Mobius strip cannot be separated; they show up together, one side, then the next, twisting and turning into each other. I began to understand that not showing up and owning all parts of my Mobius-like self could create blind spots and negatively affect others and my effectiveness as a leader.

Turning the Corner: Benefits of Vulnerability

Throughout my time learning to be a heart-led leader, vulnerability unfolded in me ever so slowly, and the willingness to engage in personal reflection got me there. As Procee (2006), states, "reflection in education is a field full of promises: promises for improving professional proficiency, for fostering personal growth, and for increasing social justice" (p. 252). Reflection was the promise to myself to allow vulnerability in. The more I learned about myself as a person, the more I was able to understand myself as an educator and leader. I started to think about how I wanted to respond to people and situations, and I came to realize that I actually valued vulnerability in others. If this was what I valued, how could I not model it for others? As Brown (2012) explains, "we love seeing raw truth and openness in other people, but we are afraid to let them see it in us" (p. 41).

I needed people to know who I was authentically in order to build solid relational trust. To become that person, I had to be vulnerable, which also included being willing to say *I need your help. I can't do it alone*. Sometimes being vulnerable meant opening up, and then letting others provide input and ideas, or allowing a pause and letting others fill the space before I provide a response. This was especially important when I worked as a literacy and task design specialist. I came into others' classrooms to teach, to model good practice, and to coach teachers. By allowing others to fill the space, to guide the conversation, I was able to truly model effective leadership. I wasn't telling them what I would do, I was waiting to hear what they would do, then working with them to tweak their practice to improve. Although it was a difficult habit to break, I learned that I didn't have to have all the answers—which is good because I never really did to begin with! I realized that I needed to be fully present to notice when I wasn't giving others the time to speak, to get my ego out of the way, and give others an opportunity to find their voices too.

Additionally, learning how to be in the moment allowed me to listen better to others, and to take a pause before I responded. Being fully present in the moment is probably one of the most important skills I have learned as a leader. I cannot do three things at once and still be effective. I have to fully engage with conversations, to the point where we have a rotating minute taker, as I have realized even that simple task of recording really limits my ability to engage fully. Being fully present, giving all of my attention and focus to a conversation, helps engage others and brings us together. Reflecting on my past and present, I see the difference in the teams I work with when I, and my team, are fully present. In the past, trying to multi-task led to the need for repeat conversations, frustration, and a dysfunctional team. Now, being more fully present during our team conversations has changed our dynamic. We listen to each other. We hash out ideas more fully. We leave more positive, knowing what our next steps are. Leading a team that is invited to the present moment has improved my ability to lead the important work we do in schools more effectively and efficiently.

Being authentic, open, and approachable are part of being vulnerable. I sometimes feel intimidated by people whom I deem as too perfect: I think that they have so many glaring strengths, that they won't accept me and my faults, and so I hide. In the early years of my career I never took my problems or challenges to leaders, as I didn't want to be seen as weak. However, when I started working with leaders who were willing to be vulnerable, my views changed. I observed that being vulnerable and letting down one's guard helped to build relationships because people seem more relatable, more human. When a principal I worked with came to a staff meeting and apologized to the staff, I was blown away. I had never seen a leader do this, but the feedback from staff revealed they appreciated her honesty and humility in admitting she was wrong. More than anything, people were willing to forgive her, recognizing that a leader is human too. Being vulnerable, and willing to let others see the authentic person behind the leadership role front, can be a tool for others' self-development. Observing other leaders model vulnerability showed me the way on this journey.

Vulnerability as Self-Care

Vulnerability has become my way to practice self-care: "Everyday life shows abundant evidence that without this purposeful, intentional, vulnerability, human life does not flourish fully" (Bruni & Tufano, 2017, p. 408). For me, finding a way to be vulnerable and make connections with others in a way that feels comfortable has allowed me to flourish. In the past, I have censored myself to try to make others happy. But now, being vulnerable means that, while my thoughts and ideas might be in conflict with others, I am also able to better hold a space for these differences and still share my voice. Feeling the relief of disclosing myself to others and not experiencing a negative consequence has resulted in less fear in my life, which was needed to end the pattern of self-silencing.

I've also found that by showing compassion for myself and creating a space for my voice, I have been better able to create a safe space for others to do the same. Opening myself to vulnerability has relieved me of a great deal of stress that I didn't know I was carrying. In the past, I focused on keeping people out by not being open with who I was and how I felt. Vulnerability has allowed me to admit mistakes, gain forgiveness, and enjoy social interactions without worry, enhancing better mental health (Bruk, Scholl, & Bless, 2018). Although we seem to believe that being vulnerable will somehow make people like us less, research shows that being vulnerable often improves people's perception of us: "when it comes to others, individuals seem to view the act of showing vulnerability rather as showing strength and as a desirable behavior" (Burk et al., 2018, p. 194).

Modern society places many expectations on women to be more aware of others' needs and to place those needs before our own (Beauboeuf-Lafontant, 2007), and this is particularly true of educators. As an independent woman, it is difficult to ask for support. I still feel at times that I need to prove that I can do it on my own, particularly as I move into more formal leadership roles. Women, including myself, often self-silence, and hide important aspects of their lives from those around them out of fear of how these aspects will, or won't, be accepted (Beauboeuf-Lafontant, 2007). Being vulnerable has allowed me to break this habit. It has forced me to recognize how silencing myself to make others more comfortable is detrimental to my own self-expression and empowerment.

In the past, I often silenced myself in professional situations, assuming others knew better than me, and I didn't want to rock the boat. However, this is changing. At a recent staff meeting, it was suggested by our leader that we post a long, wordy, very adult quote in a space reserved for our students. It was a quote that had no meaning for our students, and it didn't seem to represent their collective voice. During the staff meeting, the discomfort in everyone's eyes was clear, but no one spoke up. Mustering my courage, I finally spoke up. I was respectful and polite, and I spoke the truth I saw. Others approached me later and thanked me. As a learning leader, you support your leadership team, work together, and create opportunities where everyone has input into creating ideas. In this example, no one had heard the proposed quote ahead of time. Additionally, no one had an opportunity to make suggestions that would reflect the voice of students. Part of being a leader is also knowing when it is essential to speak up, especially for students, and to be willing to be the one to make those hard statements. I am grateful for the ability to be more vulnerable and skillful in taking these kinds of risks.

Being vulnerable has also allowed me to respond to my emotions in a more helpful way. There have been times when being emotionally vulnerable has proven fruitful, even though it was not easy. Once I cried in front of my boss. And I mean ugly cried. Disappointed in not getting a promotion, and upset by the look of pity I *thought* I was receiving, all of my emotions came tumbling out. However, from this incident arose one of the best—and perhaps hardest—conversations of my educational career. I had two choices. I could brush it off or I could dig deeper into why I didn't get the job. By choosing to have this difficult conversation, I opened myself up to hear both the good and the bad about what others were seeing in me at that time. I listened. I really listened. It was hard to hear, but I painfully recognised the truth. This experience made me aware that I could be better and that this moment was a place I could learn and grow from. Being vulnerable enough to have this conversation and to share my feelings of disappointment was a form of self-care: it opened me up to hear my inner self speak the truth, and to take the appropriate and necessary steps to improve. Hiding from my true self is self-harm, leaving me like a closed bud, full of potential, yet unable to grow. Owning the places where I need improvement allows me to affirm the strengths that can be utilized to propel myself forward. I am grateful that I care enough about myself to do this vulnerable work.

Mindfulness

Not every emotional encounter is going to result in a life-changing conversation. Having presented myself as being a strong person for so long, it took a lot to realize that I didn't need to be strong all the time. Importantly, I started bringing mindfulness practices into my own life and work. I began to allow, accept, and understand my emotions, which in turn helped me to manage them more skillfully. I use mindful breathing to successfully address stressful conversations. I am better able to share difficult things with people, while being aware of my emotions and being able to manage them more effectively. These are essential skills for leaders. Stressful and difficult conversations happen daily, be it upset parents, injured students, or frustrated teachers, so leaders need to be able to have these conversations in a mindful way that calms a situation. Being mindfully present with the inhale and exhale of my breath makes it more likely that I will respond, not react, as well as listen and accept, and not dismiss others' comments or ideas even though I don't agree with them. Mindfulness helps me manage the difficult conversations as I work with more calm and focus alongside teachers, supporting their growth, guiding our meetings, and inspiring change and innovation in our school community.

Mindfulness practice is not something that comes easily for me, but my practice has been improving. Sometimes I have a formal mindfulness meditation first thing in the morning, and at other times I engage in informal practices. Connecting with the earth during walks or in my garden, I am able to be thankful and grounded. I often stop to pause and see the beauty of the plants thriving in my classroom, the mountains on my drive into work, or the house I worked so hard to finally purchase. I create mindfulness in the little moments that I have learned to become more aware of throughout the day. I also practice mindfulness by taking a few deep breaths to find the calm before responding, when expressing my gratitude, or when slowing down to take in a beautiful moment. As a person who struggles to slow down, noticing the little things feels like a victory. I have also used mindfulness to change my expectations for myself. I notice the thoughts of perfection peeking through, and then adjust my priorities and expectations of myself (Gillespie & Temple, 2011), which reduces my anxiety considerably.

Vulnerable Courage

Recently, I utilized an exciting opportunity in order to learn how to further build my vulnerability as a learning leader in a new school setting. I transitioned to a new school where no one knew me, and this somehow made it feel safer for me to ask for help from others. This new setting was an important aspect of my continuing journey with vulnerability. Other educators were able to get to know me without any preconceived notions about who I was, how I would act, or what I was like; thus, I had the chance for a fresh start, which included showing up as my true self from day one. I stopped hiding. I felt lighter and more approachable. Most importantly, vulnerability allowed myself to be the person I am, not what I think others want me to be. I gave myself permission to show up as myself, which I continue to practice every day. Affirming myself in this way has been very empowering. Of course, I am still a work in progress, and there are days that old habits creep back in. However, those days are fewer and fewer. The habits that stem from my mindfulness practice keep me grounded and vulnerable.

It took courage to become a vulnerable heart-led leader. Through opening my heart to vulnerability, I was able to take a step forward and show up more often as my true self. Finding a safe circle of other educators who were also willing to be vulnerable was crucial in helping me find my way as a more authentic leader. Today, I embrace my vulnerability, which includes the ability to share this story with the hope that others may also risk affirming and embracing the gifts that vulnerability has to offer them too.

References

Beauboeuf-Lafontant, T. (2007). You have to show strength: An exploration of gender, race, and depression. *Gender & Society, 21*(1), 28–51. https://doi.org/10.1177/0891243206294108

Brown, B. (2017). *Braving the wilderness: The quest for true belonging and the courage to stand alone.* New York: Random House.

Brown, B. (2012). *Daring greatly: How the courage to be vulnerable transforms the way we live, love, parent, and lead.* New York: Gotham Books.

Brown, B. (June, 2010). *The power of vulnerability.* Retrieved from https://ted.com/talks/brene_brown_the_power_of_vulnerability?language=en.

Brown, B., Friesen, S., & Marcotte, C. (2017). *Mid-level learning leaders driving innovation in schools.* Paper presented to the American Educational Research Association (AERA), April 27-May 1, San Antonio, TX.

Bruk, A., Scholl, S., & Bless, H. (2018). Beautiful mess effect: Self–other differences in evaluation of showing vulnerability. *Journal of Personality and Social Psychology, 115*(2), 192–205. https://doi.org/10.1037/pspa0000120

Bruni, L., & Tufano, F. (2017). The value of vulnerability: The transformative capacity of risky trust. *Judgement & Decision Making, 12*(4), 408–414. Retrieved from: http://web.a.ebscohost.com.ezproxy.lib.ucalgary.ca/ehost/detail/detail?vid=0&sid=19d594db43ab488f93aa3f8d4d-600ba5%40sessionmgr4006&bdata=JnNpdGU9ZWhvc3Qtb-Gl2ZQ%3d%3d#AN=124449342&db=a9h

Gillespie, B., & Temple, H. (2011). Seeking the new perfect. *ABA Journal, 97*(7), 29–30. Retrieved from: http://web.a.ebscohost.com.ezproxy.lib.ucalgary.ca/ehost/detail/detail?vid=0&sid=dfc1c56cae484d498052ad-32c857f558%40sessionmgr4008&bdata=JnNpdGU9ZWhvc3Qtb-Gl2ZQ%3d%3d#AN=63570385&db=bth

Palmer, P. (2004). *A hidden wholeness: The journey towards the undivided life.* San Francisco, CA: Jossey-Bass.

Procee, H. (2006). Reflection in education: A Kantian epistemology. *Educational Theory, 58*(3), 237–253. https://doi.org/10.1111/j.1741-5446.2006.00225.x

Chapter 2

Heart Beats: Finding a Rhythm of Self-Care in Education

Rob Chrol

"I don't trust people who don't love themselves and tell me, 'I love you.' ... There is an African saying which is: Be careful when a naked person offers you a shirt."

(Maya Angelou, 1997).

I appreciate the wisdom of Maya Angelou, whose thoughts and feelings about life, love, and leadership have been a lighthouse educationally and personally. This particular quote appeared at a rather challenging time in my life, and has a cheeky quality that has resonated with me strongly ever since. *You can not give what you do not have.* While conceptually this seems completely logical and obvious, it feels less clear when I apply this to myself and my inner resources; after all, do I not have an endless amount of energy to give? Surely it can not be true that I might run out of care for the people I lead. I have come to learn that while the care doesn't run out, my ability to offer it in a sustainably healthy way is most definitely finite.

I am a high school music educator, as well as a teacher-leader. Lambert (2003) describes teacher-leaders as "those whose dreams of making a difference have been kept alive or have been reawakened by engaging with colleagues and working within a professional culture" (p. 33). Additionally, teacher-leaders accept responsibility for student learning, have a strong sense of self, are open to learning, and are committed to improving their schools (Lambert, 2003). I have been engaged in leadership actions my whole career as a teacher. This includes engaging constructively in staff meetings, offering unique perspectives during conversations, sharing ideas and practices with others, and striving to support people through challenges. I also support the broader vision in my school and community, which has led to new opportunities as well as more defined leadership roles: school leadership team, leading professional development for other educators, and becoming the student voice coordinator for my school division.

This chapter will describe how I am able to keep my dream of making a difference alive as a teacher-leader, from a heart-led perspective, as I prepare for and advance into educational leadership. "In the same way that one is born to learn, everyone is born to lead" (Lambert, 2003, p. 33). However, building leadership capacity must be intentional and be supported through opportunities for skillful development in areas related to personal/self-leadership, culture leadership, and team leadership (Valdez & Ikemoto, 2015). Specifically, this chapter will show how developing the skills for leadership through practices that invite the resources of the heart positively impacted my ability as a teacher-leader to advance personal, cultural, and team leadership.

I believe that I provide leadership by the way I think, speak, and act in every context, and so awareness of the quality of my actions is paramount. As a teacher-leader, I *think* and *plan* ahead to what my school and community will need for sustainable success. I need to also *speak* mindfully, and choose my words intentionally to uplift myself, others, or a situation. Additionally, a teacher-leader *acts* assertively and kindly, drawing from the heart of courage within. While this vision may appear to be a tall order, I believe that it is also attainable.

I searched for a long time to find a graduate program that could help prepare me as a leader and sustain my teacher-leader spark. Finally, I found an interdisciplinary degree with a shared focus on fostering healthy and just schools and leading with heart, which was exactly the right fit. In retrospect, at some point in my eleven-year journey as a teacher-leader, by engaging in habit-based mindless work practices and frenzied activity, I ran out of tenacity. I began to also run out of heart, and I needed to find a way to keep my teacher-leader spark alive.

Learning to lead with heart has given me three specific gifts: the ability to understand with compassion my own and others' beliefs and actions; the knowledge and ability to design environments and interactions where my own and others' self-care is nurtured; and an appreciation and acceptance of my own and others' light and shadow. These will be discussed in the upcoming sections. I have always led and learned from the perspective of a music maker and educator, and this chapter is organised in a way that is reflective of who I am. That, in and of itself, represents a big learning for me as a leader: my offerings resonate most authentically when shared in the narrative of my experience.

Lessons from the Woodshed: Reframing Personal Leadership

For me, chopping wood in the woodshed is a metaphor for the hard work and labour needed to survive. All achievement comes in partnership with effort—but the woodshed also has unintended consequences. An overreliance on this view led me to believe that the sole path to improvement was work hard, and if that didn't work then I need to work harder still. Being a teacher-leader can be an energy black hole as I contend with both the responsibilities of the classroom along with broader issues and activities. I perceived my compulsion to put in more time (I used to call this work ethic) as an admirable strength on which to double down, but others could easily identify it as a professional blind spot that limited my effectiveness, actually doing more harm than good (Bunting, 2016).

Through a skewed vision of what effective work actually was, I was exhausting myself. My situation felt a bit like sitting in a leaky boat. Bailing water became my goal when I should have been asking better questions like: "What do I need to plug the holes?" My *holes* in this case were the ways that I let fearful and unhelpful thoughts of inadequacy drive my beliefs and actions. I tired myself out by continuously trying harder to keep these feelings down, instead of exploring them with a curiosity that could render them less powerful. I hid my blind spots, not realizing that talking openly about them and inviting those around me to reflect mine back to me, actually enhances authenticity in leadership (George, McLean, & Craig, 2008).

I've mentioned the idea of blind spots a couple of times, so it may be helpful to say what it means to me. Primarily I mean them to be weaknesses within myself which I erroneously consider to be strengths (e.g., the work ethic example from before), or perhaps actual strengths I've considered to be weaknesses and therefore not embraced (e.g., the idea of vulnerability). I experienced first-hand how helpful owning and sharing my blind spots can be for myself and others. During a recent professional development workshop I led for K to 12 music educators, I was nervous and feeling uncomfortably vulnerable—even though I knew them all personally. The perfectionist musician in me wanted all those woodshed hours to result in a perfect performance. Instead, I took a deep breath and began with a confession of my discomfort, acknowledging that my *being human* and nervous was natural. I talked openly that day about my own compulsive work habits and compromises to my physical and emotional health. Afterwards, I was surprised when several teachers approached me to share their feelings of overwhelm, perfectionism, and fear of owning their blind spots. I smiled at the irony of it all: shining a light on my blind spots actually made it safer for others to do the same, connecting us in a courageous and more authentic way. That day I learned that through letting go and not hiding, I invite authenticity for myself and others.

Through exploring my heart, I've also reflected upon how my experience as a man may have influenced my perception of blind spots as failings. It is very common for men to struggle with self-doubt and feelings of failure considering the societal expectations that men be perceived as independent, capable, and strong. In his work on masculinity, Porter (2010) refers to these expectations as the *man box*: a space where there is no room for vulnerability. While I have felt the truth of this, I am also mindful that my choices need not be influenced by society's expectations of my maleness. Being uncomfortable with blind spots and experiencing self-doubt are human—not gendered—experiences. It is important to understand how our experience of struggle is influenced by societal norms, but I have also found through conversations with colleagues that we share these experiences, regardless of gender.

Considering my blind spots compassionately, I have learned how to honour my *light spots*, the areas of strengths and refined skills of which I am actively aware, and of which I am proud. During my training in heart-led leadership, I was invited to explore these opposing themes using a Mobius strip as a way to see that we, "can't have light without shadows" (Center for Courage and Renewal & Francis, 2018, p. 63). In this activity, I named my strengths, skills, and abilities on one side of a strip of paper, and I named the parts of myself that I tend to hide—the blind spots—on the other side. On a Mobius strip, these blind spots are quite visible. In fact, they appear in conjunction with the light spots, alternating back and forth throughout the winding strip of paper. This activity revealed how awareness, and acceptance, of both sides can stop the illusion of hiding. Ironically, learning how to embrace my imperfections has made the truth of being imperfect and human much more manageable. I don't have to be perfect at anything to be a good leader.

Throughout my training as a heart-led leader, I found it easier and easier to stop chopping wood and just let go through the practice of mindfulness. Mindfulness has been a helpful tool in teaching me to *just be* at work. It has also become a regular part of my own teaching. *Mindful Mondays* are a time for my learners and I to dive deeper into specific practices, as well as the neuroscience of mindfulness. One Monday I got to practice *just being* when I was feeling overwhelmed by to-do lists. Instead of starting the usual ensemble warm up, I sat with my grade 11/12 band and said, with both defeat and acceptance in my voice, "What do all y'all do when you're just not having it anymore?" We shared a knowing laugh and had an honest conversation about strategies to feel more grounded, present, and capable when pressures rise.

I realized first-hand how my students could benefit from my own openness, personal practices, and self-care tools like mindfulness. Together, we also learned to notice and lean into positive moments as a way of honouring our *light spots*. Hanson (2018) highlights the value of the H.E.A.L. process when experiencing something positive: *Have* the experience; *Enrich* it by staying in the experience longer; *Absorb* it by really sensing it, and how it makes you feel; and *Link* it when appropriate to a past negative experience, a very effective practice that can help us keep our balance while living our Mobius strip lives.

In learning to be a heart-led teacher-leader I was invited to partner with my heart to resource and equip me to deal with the challenges within myself (Mitchell-Pellett, 2018). Though the process of self-exploration initially felt uncomfortable, I learned to consider myself as worthy of compassion and curiosity. I could look back on those years of bailing water with understanding, warmth, and self-forgiveness. I began to see myself as a person first and teacher-leader second. This was a huge reframing for me: As an advocate for my own justice and care, I have the power to choose my perspective on every situation in a way that elevates me (D. Jones, personal communication, July 12, 2018). This focus on learning how to reconnect to and accept my humanness with self-compassion and care was critical to developing personal leadership that cultivated practices for continual improvement. This process also helped build my capacity to facilitate opportunities for others to explore, value, and share their inner resources, which I will describe in the upcoming section.

Harmony: Cultivating Community-Care and Justice

A well-crafted melody is beautiful. Pure and intent all on its own, a melody can tell a story and convey emotion one pitch at a time with stunning efficiency. However, melody can also be thin, presented from only one perspective, lacking both depth and context. Harmony on the other hand, is the addition of different but supporting voices simultaneously, which enhances the story of melody, creating a powerful energy that melody alone cannot accomplish. If melody is self-care, harmony is community-care—the coming together of multiple voices in a shared intention to support wellbeing for all. Having brought heart-led leadership practices into my work and life, I have noticed a clear improvement in my ability to support changes in school culture and facilitate team leadership.

In many public schools, student voice and wellbeing have not been given the attention they need. There is mounting concern with how practices established within a school culture can lead to the oppression of student voice and agency. There is a tendency to put the blame of poor performance upon students, instead of involving students in the process of changing curriculum and instruction through inviting their participation (Mitra, 2003). To change perpetuating actions entrenched in school cultures that negate student voice, we need to help students cultivate personal leadership and apply their skills and gifts in meaningful contexts, enhancing their ability to create worthwhile experiences and change.

Through my role as a teacher-leader, I was invited to help develop student leaders in our school division. This opportunity evolved from a high school credit course I designed called *Music Leadership*. The course was intended to help students experience connections between musicianship and leadership. I facilitated with students many of the *leading with heart* activities that I had learned, which supported authentic identity development, self-awareness and self-reflection, and compassionate interactions with others. Working first to strengthen their own melodies, students learned to weave their voices togethers in the harmony of community-care. Classes began with a check-in where students shared how they were feeling, as well as stories of success or frustration. Learning how to find and use one's voice through sharing, listening intently, and practicing compassionate responding to others were key experiences. We worked to build calm and focused attention through short breathing exercises, and we practiced mindful listening by focusing on various musical sounds.

Additionally, students practiced applying their leadership skills in the real world through our weekly visits to the early-years school, where each teenager mentored one or more *buddies* in a grade 1/2 class. Their work together alternated between music learning and classroom learning, composing songs while connecting to work in other classes. Students discovered new things about themselves, finding confidence in their shared leadership and designing effective learning experiences for others. One grade 2 student declared his new success on the monkey bars was because his music-buddy helped him be brave. A group of grade 1 students took it upon themselves to teach the kindergarten class how to be band conductors because, "We're musicians and musicians share." High schoolers with a tendency to disengage were nurturing and attentive role models to the younger students. To call it magical doesn't even begin to describe the powerful learning experiences that students led for one another.

Along with building self-awareness and leadership skills, students also learned the importance of caring for a community of others. After each visit to the grade 1/2 class, the teenagers would reflect together on the session they just had with the younger students. During one class a student stated, "I have some work to do." Believing that he was talking about his younger buddy, I asked for clarification. The response was not what I expected. The student answered, "My buddy thinks he is terrible at drawing, and really just terrible in general, and that makes me sad because he's so young to be so self-critical. I was about that age when I first started beating up on myself and you know, it's just grown worse over the years. I guess if I want to help my buddy, I have to learn to be nicer to myself first. I have to show my buddy how." I thanked the student for sharing such a powerful personal realisation, and as a class we acknowledged how hard it can be to show kindness and compassion to ourselves. The students learned from their peer's story how self-care prepares them to care for others more authentically—melody contributing to harmony. In response, I redesigned our weekly assignments and had students reflect on how to deal with challenging feelings, compassionately noticing the unhelpful thoughts and letting them go through non-attachment. Working with students to develop self-leadership taught me as a teacher-leader how to be responsive to their needs and unique voices, develop their strengths, and help them build resources through the practice of mindfulness—all critical elements of self-leadership.

One year after the development of Music Leadership, I was invited by my superintendent to help reconfigure a divisional student council into a Student Voice group, which provided an opportunity for culture leadership. Culture leadership involves "building a learning orientation among team members and students who are focused on ... personal responsibility for their own development. Creating a set of expectations ... to get a set of behaviors ... that builds the culture of effective student achievement" (Valdez & Ikemoto, 2015, p. 14). Within my division, the element of culture that was prioritized for improvement was enhancing student voice in support of wellbeing and achievement. I was honoured to be tasked with providing leadership for the facilitation of this program.

The Student Voice group was composed of high school students from three distinct towns. We met four times over the school year to provide opportunities for students to develop agency and authentic voice. Previously, our divisional student council planned events for students, but didn't sufficiently enhance student participation or voice in a meaningful way. It was hoped that this new Student Voice group would give students opportunities to discuss issues from a variety of perspectives, collaborate, foster engagement amongst peers, and share their ideas and needs with administration and teachers. My role was to design and facilitate these four sessions. The students who attended the sessions were accompanied by their principals and one or both of the superintendents, and so it was important to also engage these adults in the process of developing self-awareness, agency, and voice for our students. I structured the sessions very similarly to Music Leadership, building on the skills and concepts inherent in leading with heart.

Through mindful listening of their inner voices, students and administrators reflected on their personal beliefs, values, gifts, and strengths, and how these inner resources could help them support their school and community. They explored how knowing their strengths (light), and addressing their areas for growth (shadow), were foundational for knowing themselves, having an authentic voice, and helping others. One student remarked at how she needed to set aside her desire to be liked by peers to effectively lead a successful *No-Phones Wellbeing Challenge* at her school, despite initial resistance to the idea.

I tried to facilitate a community of leaders, where all voices were heard, by modeling phrases and questions that fostered deeper listening and understanding. For example, we practiced using phrases such as: "I appreciate what you are sharing"; "I'd like to extend that idea"; "What you just said makes me wonder about _____"; or "That's a very different perspective from what I have experienced." This practice engendered community-care with a reminder that each person had valuable wisdom to share and was a respected member of the team.

I was nervous as I began working with the Student Voice group, putting pressure on myself to do a good job in the presence of my administrators. Feelings of self-doubt and insecurity flared when the expectations I put on myself as the leader were unreasonable. Was I prepared enough? Was I engaging and charismatic enough? How would they view me?

I later realized that my thoughts of feeling incapable were just thoughts. I give credit to the practice of mindfulness, which helped me detach from these unhelpful thinking patterns. I was able to apply Hanson's (2018) *bringing in the good* practices, countering the negative thoughts with the truth that I am enough: I have the gifts, strengths, and positive inner experiences held within, to help facilitate work with others as a teacher-leader.

Every student, principal, and superintendent involved with the Student Voice group worked together with integrity and genuine care, changing the culture related to student voice in our division. Students were afforded more consistent ways to offer direct feedback on teaching and learning practices, helping to co-create a teaching and learning framework used throughout the division. Students also became more active leaders in their schools, designing messages and educational experiences connected to wellbeing—an important consideration, both for our division and the province as a whole. Additionally, it was formalized that a student representative would attend the Board of Trustees meetings, providing student voice and perspective in the division.

The work from this divisional team even influenced the practice of supporting student voice and agency in my own school community. When the construction of a new music room for our students was cancelled at the government level, students were particularly disappointed as they had waited years for this space. In response, I teamed with my colleagues to create a space for students to voice their concerns.

Students had many questions related to "why" the music room project was cancelled, which led to rich discussions about the democratic process, the complexity of government decisions, and the right of citizens to use their voice to ask questions for clarification. The students formed a working group, and over 10 weeks spoke to elected representatives, ran awareness campaigns, and engaged community members. They organised a letter-writing campaign, gathering over 500 letters of support asking the government respectfully for reconsideration. An invitation to question period at the Manitoba Legislature followed where the issue was raised directly with the Premier. This hard work eventually paid off when the music room project was reinstated! This was a powerful experience for both students and our adult community as we learned how to effectively take a stand to address a collective need.

The experience taught me how to better navigate others' emotional challenges while supporting a team dedicated to making a difference. The opportunity to practice facilitative leadership skills in support of others' goals considerably enhanced my growth as a team leader (Valdez & Ikemoto, 2015). A large part of my role involved creating a space for student voice to arise, while helping them access heart-led leadership skills. We had constructive conversations about how to make sense of what was unfolding. Students were reminded that they could use their attentive resources to notice difficult emotions, applying skillful means of dealing with them; for example, sharing their voices and perspectives, which is an act of self-justice (Prilleltensky, 2012). The adults in our school community modeled healthy emotional intelligence by reminding students to hold their passion with effective, thoughtful, and heartful actions. We learned how to work in a spirit of partnership and good will, even though not everyone was in agreement throughout the process.

Throughout, I drew on my self-care practices of trusting in my beliefs and values, recognising blind spots, and validating my own worth and feelings, to ensure that I could care for my community in a tempered, thoughtful, and strengthening way. This helped me better support my community in pursing justice—a balance between what was owed to others and what they themselves were owed (Sheppard, Lewicki, & Minton, 1992). Leading with my heart gave the students permission to lead with theirs. As a community, we learned how collective leadership, which included both students and adults, could leverage stronger collective efficacy. We had all grown tall and strong in the soil of a community committed to shared leadership and care for one another.

There is Still Music

Two years into my journey, I am still discovering new things about myself every day. Self-care is now something I consider a professional responsibility—a requirement for me to be most effective. I see my community through different eyes, wishing for them the same health and wellbeing I want and need for myself. I am especially grateful for how this learning has taught me to reframe my perspective on the woodshed. I was working so hard, giving so much, and completely losing track of my melody in the cacophony of the job. There was no music, only noise. I believed I needed to sacrifice my wellness to prove my worth. That was wrong. Now, through leaning into heart-based practices, I value myself more, working slower with more intention. This journey has helped me acknowledge that I am worthy of treating myself in a more just manner. The resulting harmony has improved my ability to be in concert with my community immeasurably. I cannot imagine humming along any other way.

References

Center for Courage & Renewal & Francis, S. L. (2018). *The courage way: Leading and living with integrity*. Oakland, CA: Berrett-Koehler.

George, B., McLean, A., & Craig, N. (2008). *Finding your true north: A personal guide*. San Francisco, CA: Wiley.

Hanson, R. (2018). *Resilient: How to grow an unshakable core of calm, strength, and happiness*. New York, NY: Harmony Books.

Lambert, L. (2003). *Leadership capacity for lasting school improvement*. Alexandria, VA: Association for Supervision and Curriculum Development.

Porter, T. (2010, December). *A call to men* [Video file]. Retrieved from https://www.ted.com/talks/tony_porter_a_call_to_men

Prilleltensky, I. (2012). Wellness as fairness. *American Journal of Community Psychology*, June. DOI 10.1007/s10464-011-9448-8

Sheppard, B., Lewicki, R., & Minton, J. (1992). *Organizational justice: The search for fairness in the workplace*. New York, NY: Maxwell Macmillan.

Valdez, M., & Ikemoto, G. (2015). The Research Behind Untapped: An Evaluation of a New Leaders' Emerging Leaders Program [PDF file]. Retrieved from https://newleaders.org/wp-content/uploads/2016/09/Untapped_Research.pdf

Williamson, M. (1996). *A return to love: Reflections on the principles of "A course in miracles"*. New York, NY: HarperCollins.

Chapter 3

Conflict and the Path To Wholeheartedly Embracing Leadership

Jacqueline E.K Cameron

Healer, heal thyself; Leader, lead thyself
- unknown

This chapter is a brief synopsis of how I came to honour the wisdom found in reclaiming and connecting to my inner self, as informed by the convergent timelines of becoming a new mother, working on my M.Ed., and stepping into a formal leadership role (after shirking it for many years!). Through a process of reacquainting myself with my authentic identity, gifts, and perspectives, I was able to get out of my own way and tap into both my heart and efficacy as a leader. I use the term *authentic self* interchangeably with the term *self* in this chapter to mean the person who is purely me, or, how Frederick Buechner (1993) explains it, "the place where your deep gladness meets the world's deep need" (p.119). 'She' who can exist with no added narrative (whether it be externally or internally imposed), who accepts her strength and gifts, lends self-compassion towards her faults, and who operates from a place of intrinsic heart-led knowing and vocation.

Uncovering the authentic self starts with self-care, which naturally leads to self-justice. Self-justice is being able to embrace the fact that we all deserve to understand and live from a place of integrity, joy, curiosity, sincerity, passion, creativity, fulfillment, and a feeling of wholeness. It is the acceptance of who I am, and it is allowing myself to show up as I am in the world. Tending to my mind, heart, and body through mindfulness practices has led to finding self-justice by honouring my right to be here, and to find my personal seat of power. Not power in the sense of muscle, brawn, and domination, but power as strength, wisdom, and self-awareness, paired with compassion towards others. Cultivating self-care and self-justice were foundational in informing me how to serve the other—the collective—with integrity and social justice as I figured out my place in the world of leadership.

My Story

My story, regardless of how ferociously I once wanted to believe otherwise, has value. We all have a story, a narrative imprinted upon us which includes how we view and value the self. Part of my story was that I believed that I wasn't worthy enough to fully step into and embrace my strengths. It's a common human story, actually, although we all don't always have the grit to talk about it in public. As a teacher of fifteen years, a spouse to my husband, and a mother to two young children, these last five years have provided me with opportunities and challenges, both welcomed and uninvited, to dig into my personal narrative and reconnect with my authentic self. Through compassionate acts of self-care, which includes putting in the necessary work to know myself, I open opportunities to be of authentic service to others by being me. Just plain old me! I have the right to be me, and in doing so, I offer a unique perspective and way of being that can serve others. I didn't always feel this way. Yet, I have come to the realization that all the paradoxical parts of shadow and light, of wounds and gifts, are interwoven into a unique human being that can effectively help others.

There was a period within these last years, while I lived my life as an entirely misleading outward package, during which one would never know I struggled with a sense of having lost connection to my authentic self and my place in the world. The experience was amplified by postpartum depression and anxiety, which ended up being both an unlikely gift and a pivotal season of my life. Through the fog of therapy, medications, heartbreak, heart-openings, and an animal-like fight to be present for my newborn daughter, I was provided with an amazing opportunity: to understand the darkness I was living under. I began to understand how the skills I relied upon to navigate that darkness were what I could identify as strengths. I eventually was able to intentionally alchemize something beautiful from the bleakness I felt through the process of re-learning how to listen to my heart and inner voice.

There's a saying that I heard once: "When the dark gets dark, the light gets lighter." This was true for me. As I was piecing back together who I was and how I wanted to be in this world, an opportunity in my graduate studies programming presented itself; through it, I found a supportive cohort of colleagues that helped me strengthen the threads of self. With their support, I learned how to understand my own heart through the practice of mindfulness. While under the umbrella of educational leadership, tools such as mindfulness were presented to better understand ourselves as leaders. The practice of mindfulness facilitated a spacious container where pieces of myself that I had tucked away with reticence, could return without judgment to be acknowledged, understood, and eventually celebrated, as they brought forth great wisdom. It took me a long time to accept that the darkest parts of my narrative were resources and gems that I could offer the world, and to realize how they could inform my individual perceptions and understanding of leadership.

Who Am I to be a Leader?

Leadership skills came to me relatively naturally, yet I never actively pursued a formal leadership role within the school system. I have a curiosity and caring for others that translates into the capacity to easily form connections with people. I genuinely adore the magic of facilitating opportunities for others to find a sense of community and belonging. Teaching was a natural extension of this skill and, although several of my administrators identified and tried to nudge me towards my leadership potential, an unsettling, hide-under-the-rug mentality lingered: Who am I to be a leader? I thought it would be a conceited act to verbalize any interest in a leadership role. For reasons unknown, I had a sincere belief that I would be perceived as an imposter, undeserving, and innately ill-prepared to be in a formal leader position.

Additionally, I didn't know if I had the fortitude to deal with the responsibilities and important decisions that I observed being executed by effective leaders I respected. I had never been particularly good at playing the game and accepting systemic conventions and unspoken rules that, in my mind, did not serve the greater good. I disliked red-tape and bureaucracy and I didn't want to end up broken-hearted by not being able to affect meaningful change. I laughingly joked that managing kids was no problem but managing adults would be more of a challenge; my heart-on-my sleeve temperament would be my downfall. I had observed other leaders, and it wasn't always pretty. Some shone brightly, while others lost all their sparkle and were reduced to a dim twinkle. Some leaders formed meaningful connections to their role and colleagues, while others seemed disconnected, inauthentic, and devoid of passion.

Leadership looked messy, akin to a battle zone where the wounded were plenty. I was dragging my heels when faced with the prospect of leadership. Observing the wounds of others, and feeling my own, had left me disenchanted and hesitant to put myself in such a situation of vulnerability. I had observed large gaps between where we could be as educational professionals supporting students, teachers, and leaders, and where we actually are. The soul, for many educators, seemed detached from their role (Palmer, 1999), and many become toughened and heart-broken for a multitude of reasons— including me.

Wounds needn't be physical to cause harm. Sometimes, we don't even realize that we're carrying something in our hearts that affects how we perceive the world around us. Whether it be due to impossible policy changes, heavy emotional labour, volatile school-board economics, unhealthy tensions in the learning community, or other circumstances, many broken-hearted educators and leaders can't even identify they are wounded. There's a tension and an uneasiness revealed in our outward behaviours; however, counterintuitively, if there is an intentional desire to do so there is also a freedom to be gained. Maslin-Ostrowski & Ackerman (2000) suggest that:

> Paradoxically, the wound can also be a liberation from an unbearable situation – the juncture between an undesirable past and a desirable future. The challenge is that the wound might lead to something else, or a person might continue going through his or her wounding (p.10).

This concept of the wounded leader (Maslin-Ostrowski and Ackerman, 2000) is interesting to me, and one that I am familiar with as a teacher and emerging leader. Having poor boundaries, constantly trying to please others, or having difficulty with knowing how to resolve conflicts effectively has created issues, including blind spots and emotional triggers, for me. Knowing myself well is imperative to dealing with those issues. During conflict, the reactionary part of the brain is engaged, limiting an effective understanding of the unfolding of a situation (Goleman & Davidson, 2017). However, we can learn to respond thoughtfully to situations through practicing awareness and self-care, which fosters better emotional regulation (Goleman & Davidson, 2017). Considering my wounds, with the intent of understanding them, requires a tremendous amount of vulnerability, courage, gentleness, and self-compassion. I've come to understand a beautiful paradox: that there is space for very seemingly contradictory feelings and situations to exist. As I have discovered, a required first step in that process is to acknowledge the different facets of myself which may be in discord (inner conflict), along with friction in my outer world and experiences (external conflict).

Staying in the Seat of Conflict

Conflict, both inward and outward, is something I have had the opportunity to deeply investigate throughout my graduate coursework; coursework that included learning how to become a heart-led leader. It's an uncomfortable topic, which previously I would have instinctively shied away from. However, as a leader it is essential to understand and acknowledge that both my *being* and *doing* impacts others, as I am impacted by people, culture, and the environment around me. As a leader, my inner self, including my thoughts, emotions, and values, cannot be separated from the embodiment of what I do (my actions). That there is a gap between these two important elements is obvious given that we are fallible human beings. However, being aware of this gap and how I am being and acting in any given moment is critically important to my efficacy as a leader.

Through being informed by the (admittedly at times) difficult work of self-understanding, and actualization, and having to unveil aspects of myself I may not want to acknowledge, I am performing a very real process of self-care. Self-care is also an act of self-justice as I learn to accept and care for all the facets of myself—which are there whether I like them or not! As a new leader, I always strive to walk-my-talk and lead from a place of both strength and compassion. I continuously check-in with myself to ensure that my doing is aligned with my authentic self, so that both my inner and outer displays of self are in check, truthful, and meaningful.

> Self-care is never a selfish act - it is simply good stewardship of the only gift I have, the gift I was put on earth to offer others. Anytime we can listen to true self and give the care it requires, we do it not only for ourselves, but for the many others whose lives we touch. (Parker Palmer, 1999)

Learning how to lean into tension has been another important part of my development as a leader. Starting with learning how to identify and acknowledge the conflict between my inner self and outer actions, I also had to redevelop a new relationship with the word conflict. Prior to my graduate work, I had universally viewed conflict as a negative thing. Conflict meant instability, rupture of relationship, potential loss, and intense emotions. I have since arrived at an understanding that conflict is not only natural, it is the way we move forward—it gives me the grist or energy to move ahead. When I have felt supported and brave enough to step into the discomfort of conflict, rather than away from it, I have found the gift of deeper clarity. While not directly linked to my own leadership path, my personal experiences with mental illness contributed directly to what I am able to offer as a leader, as well as how I've chosen to lead. As my own healing occurred, I also needed to heal those dark moments in my own narrative by addressing the conflict they represented. I could have chosen to live there and be in a constant place of shame and anger, but instead, I made a healing choice; a choice to give those dark moments in my life a purpose.

Through the self-justice of shifting my perspective to one of compassion for others and self, I've been able to reframe those nightmarish moments in my narrative as gifts. Beautiful opportunities to acknowledge and better understand the humanity of myself and others deeply. While this self-care and justice was very personal, it directly contributes to how I now choose to share myself with others via leadership driven by a wish for collective wellbeing. Vulnerability, as in being able to bring my individual humanness into my leadership, is a cornerstone of my actions as a leader. I am learning as a leader to "hold tension in life-giving ways" (Center for Courage & Renewal & Francis, 2018, p.137). Coming to better understand and accept my own self has engendered humility and awareness that I share with others as they learn to manage their own growth and change. As I extend my practice of intentional self-care and reflection into all aspects of my life, I can better hold the space for others to do the same through leading by example. I'm now better able to manage the tension in conflict, and can reframe it as a gift after having learned the skills on how to manage it and see its merit:

...to open a passage to the unknown, to feel that moment, the painful perception of a change to come, a loss of identity – all of this is experienced with intensity, great distress. There are wounds that crush the soul, distort and misdirect the energy of life and there are those that prompt us to grow. There are, perhaps, necessary wounds – those that quicken consciousness, oblige us to move out of the old and into a new life, catalysts to the next stages of growth. (Maslin-Ostrowski & Ackerman, 2000, p.10).

The Role of Mindfulness

I have found mindfulness practices helpful in learning how to better process conflict and uncomfortable emotions through becoming an observer of my own mind. Habitual integration of intentional thought around compassion-building and gratitude are particularly helpful, especially in times of stress. For example, I have found Metta meditation, whereby aspirations or wishes are expressed for one's own and others' safety, health, happiness, and wellbeing, has helped me to quickly, consistently, and sincerely anchor myself back into a present-moment situation with greater clarity. Additionally, being able to check in with myself using techniques to deal with emotions, such as Kornfield's (2011) R.A.I.N process (Recognize, Acknowledge, Investigate, and Non-attachment to emotion), has helped me navigate conflict situations with more skill and ease, even ones previously considered unmanageable. Through focusing on mindful awareness and skill-building practices, I strengthened my ability to approach situations with compassion and wisdom, allowing me to lead more effectively. It has been powerful to learn how to reframe my perspectives and suspend my judgment in order to be able to better listen to and understand a situation. I have learned that I am able to work in a space of duality and paradox, such as comfort and discomfort, or ease and distress.

Mindfulness practice has helped me to engender and align positive qualities of being and doing. For example, I can calmly deal with difficult situations, such as an emotional parent, teacher, or student, by approaching others with compassion, curiosity, and non-judgment. I help to create and hold a space for others to have their own process. I take things less personally. Most importantly, I've also adopted the mindset of being the host to another's difficult situation, instead of becoming the hero, swooping in to fix it all. By helping others process conflict, this provides them an opportunity to find clarity and grow their own resources. I find that this is an extraordinarily difficult shift in mindset, especially as someone who works in a compassion-based profession such as education. I have learned to allow the space for others to better understand themselves through a conflict/learning opportunity and realize that I do not need to fix things for others in order to feel effective as a leader and person. It has become apparent to me that my worth actually comes from my ability to guide and host others in their own opportunities for self-clarity and understanding: to hold the space.

Coming Full Circle

As an emerging leader, my role is to facilitate the growth and success of others and myself, with the end result being the betterment of involved stakeholders (Hanson, 2018). Getting out of my own way, by accepting all parts of myself in order to provide authentic and meaningful leadership for those involved, is necessary for creating a trusting and effective collaboration. I am working on creating leadership that is an invitation for others to courageously acknowledge and access their own leadership capacities.

My vision for effective leadership includes being seated at a table with many others. Setting the table, as the host, would entail creating the intention and setting the tone for the gathering to be productive and respectful. As the leader or host, I welcome and encourage others to sit at the table and share with intention and thoughtfulness. Some may need to establish a sense of trust and safety before joining in, while others may be more boisterous and chattier, and may need to learn how to give space to others' voices. Some may be excited to be at the table, while others may be hesitant, resentful, or fearful. As the host, when conversations lag, become heated, or devolve in an unproductive way, it is my job to nurture and support interactions so that all feel heard and valued.

Through training to become a heart-led leader, I feel my *being* (Soul) and *doing* (Role) (Palmer, 1999) are now walking together more confidently and cohesively into future leadership roles and opportunities. Now when I ask myself the question, "Who am *I* to be a Leader?", I answer myself with, "Who am I *not* to be?" I feel it in my heart. Leadership has become a deep understanding and practice of honouring and holding a space for myself and others as we learn to unearth our own gifts, with sincerity, courage, and heart.

I close with this quote from Parker Palmer (1999), which speaks to what I believe has been my ability to find those strong and true places within myself that influence my ability to face whatever comes my way as a leader, as well as my wish for others:

> We have places of fear inside of us, but we have other places as well— places with names like trust, and hope, and faith. We can choose to lead from one of those places, to stand on ground that is not riddled with the fault lines of fear, to move toward others from a place of promise instead of anxiety. As we stand in one of those places, fear may remain close at hand and our spirits may still tremble. But now we stand on ground that will support us, ground from which we can lead others toward a more trustworthy, more hopeful, more faithful way of being in the world. (p. 94)

References

Buechner, F. (1993). *Wishful thinking: A seeker's ABC*. HarperSanFrancisco.

Center for Courage & Renewal, & Francis, S. L. (2018). *The courage way: Leading and living with integrity*. Berrett-Koehler Publishers.

Goleman, D., & Davidson, R. J. (2017). *Altered traits: Science reveals how meditation changes your mind, brain, and body*. Penguin.

Hanson, R. (2018). *Resilient: How to grow an unshakable core of calm, strength, and happiness*. New York, NY: Harmony Books.

Kornfield, J. (2011). *Bringing home the Dharma: Awakening right where you are*. Boston: Shambhala Publications.

Maslin-Ostrowski, P., & Ackerman, R. H. (2000). *On being wounded: implications for school leaders*. Journal of Educational Administration, 38(3), 216–229. https://doi.org/10.1108/09578230010342240

Palmer, P. J. (1999). Let your life speak: Listening for the voice of vocation. John Wiley & Sons.

Chapter 4

A Leader Emerges from a Manager

Kimberley Dart

"There is no power greater than a community discovering what it cares about" *(Wheatley, 2002, p. 13).*

I never set out to be a leader. Like many people, I was looking for a job that I enjoyed, with challenging work, a good culture, and nice co-workers. A place where I didn't have to drag myself out of bed to go to each day. I got my first job when I was just 15-years old, and I have been employed ever since. I do not like to be *not* busy and I will try to find new projects or tasks to complete if I have free time.

I was promoted to my current management role after only 8 months with the organization. There was a lot of talk of *leadership* and *being a leader*. That was exciting to me. I wanted to do a good job and I wanted my team to be excited about our roles. It soon became apparent that despite all the talk of leadership, what they truly wanted was a *manager*—and in all fairness, that is my actual title. In my mind, leaders were inspiring: they encouraged people, and they helped people bring out their best qualities. Managers, on the other hand, tracked expenses, reviewed time off requests, and basically looked after the boring day-to-day details.

The first two years on the job were demanding. My first act was to let an employee go. This is never easy, but I think I handled it well.

A few months later, one of the senior staff left on a sudden medical leave. In the months that she was away, the spouse of another team member was diagnosed with a terminal illness, and eventually passed away. Throughout these difficult events, I was trying to build a team, was taking on extra work, and was being juggled between two supervisors. Our department was moved to a smaller space in the building. I was trying to maintain a sense of calm throughout this big change, all while onboarding new team members and working with existing team members who were angry that they no longer had private offices. The underlying stress in the workplace was so thick you could practically see it clouding the air. "Leading change is hard enough. But if you can't focus because you are overwhelmed with information and the tumult of change, you will have a hard time focusing other people's attention too…" (Powell, 2009, p.6).

I was dealing with a lot and I wanted to do a good job, both for my team and the students that we served, but I didn't feel that I had the right tools to do the job well. I tried modeling my management style after various managers and supervisors that I had worked under throughout my career, but that did not work for me. It was hard to balance the idea of *being the boss*, somewhat distant and removed from the team, and *being myself*, who wanted to jump in and be a team member. I immersed myself in becoming the best I could be in my role. I took courses that were offered internally by our Human Resources group and read books on leadership. I learned the intricacies of managing in my post-secondary environment, how to navigate our internal systems to be more effective, and how to work within the confines of the collective agreement.

While I wanted to be a leader, I had to be a manager. Too often those terms are used interchangeably when they should not be. At times I was inspiring and encouraging, and at other times I had to deny staff requests due to operational or budgetary reasons. "As a manager you need to put your company first, your team second, and your team members last" (Wermuth-Buffer, 2018, para. 8). Wermuth-Buffer's words were my reality, but it was not the reality I wanted. My team was full of great people and I wanted to bring out their best, not hinder their creativity and passion.

This inner turmoil of what I wanted and where I was created a lot of stress. I would come home exhausted at the end of the workday, I rarely slept more than five hours at night, and I lost interest in most social activities. I became irritable and was likely experiencing burnout. There was no one to talk to about my challenges: I felt like I was in this alone. I saw the talent and potential on my team, and experienced frustration at the lack of recognition for the work that we did.

Tried and Failed

Each week I met with my supervisor to report on our activities and on student engagement. Unfortunately, I felt that the conversation was one-sided. I wanted clarity on what was expected of me, but I was not getting it; as a result, I was acting based on how I *thought* they wanted me to. They seemed happy with what my team was doing and the student outcomes, but I was still unclear if I was meeting their expectations. While I was thrilled to have a boss who did not micromanage, as a new leader I was also craving direction. I felt like I was alone on an island with little hope of rescue.

In 2017, I started my master's degree. The professor told the class about servant leadership. He described it as clearing the path for your team so they can do their best work. Spears (2005) described servant leadership by saying, "True leadership emerges from those whose primary motivation is a deep desire to help others" (p. 31). I liked both descriptions, as they would allow me to turn Wermuth-Buffer's (2018) definition of leadership on its head by serving my team first. I returned to the office from class recharged and with a new energy. Immediately I scheduled a one-on-one meeting with every team member. In each meeting I asked the individual about their goals and what was getting in the way of meeting them. I made it clear that I wanted to help them and to let me know if they needed me to do anything to make their jobs easier. I had the very best of intentions. I wanted then, and now, for my team members to grow and develop as individuals and professionals. However, I unknowingly set myself along a path of resentment.

One employee took my offer very seriously. Not a week went by without an email from this person asking for something. One message might have them asking for a new whiteboard, another for tickets to an event, another to attend a conference, and so on. Unfortunately, I did not address it and it continued; in fact, it grew to the point where I would literally feel anxiety growing in me when this person's emails appeared in my inbox. Ultimately, I grew resentful, and I did not act like a leader. I would avoid interacting with this person simply to avoid their demands, and others noticed. It was not sustainable to allow that one person's requests—which I was starting to feel were like demands—to continue, neither for my mental health, our working relationship, or the team dynamic. Plans were made for a discussion, an honest conversation with this person (something that I should have done right away), but once the meeting was scheduled, they resigned.

Realistically, a person taking advantage of my offer to be there for my staff should not have become a big issue, but I turned it into one, and that had a big consequence. Because of my unseasoned leadership skills, and dislike of confrontation, I let a very small thing grow into a big thing. This led to resentment and the loss of a team member. One mistake I made was not taking the time to fully research servant leadership beyond its initial description before I acted. Someone recently told me that, "The problem is just the problem. How you react to the problem is the real problem" (Anon, 2019). My decision not to respond and address how this employee interpreted my intentions as a leader was the problem, as well as not setting effective boundaries on my end. I was trying to be the best leader I could, putting my perception of what servant leadership looked like into practice. I continued to pursue other approaches, as being an effective leader was important to me, and I was still feeling alone on my island. Servant leadership holds merit, but I know now that knowing something and doing it effectively are two independent things.

Heart-Led Leadership

When filling out the application for my master's diploma program, I dismissed a program that involved developing leadership with heart several times. This did not sound like a program that suited me. While I wanted desperately to become a good leader, I did not see value in mindfulness, nor did I understand how mindful leadership worked. I had already completed many leadership courses and came to believe that, "… authentic leadership development involves complex processes, and that it is unlikely to be achieved simply through a training program" (Avolio & Gardner, 2005, p. 322). At this point, what could another leadership class teach me? I understood the principles, but I was still looking for a way off my island. Nevertheless, I needed to find a program for my graduate studies, and I figured that I could fake my way through if I needed to. What I found was a program that introduced me to new ways of thinking, that tied together my own ideologies with proven leadership concepts, and, most surprisingly, I found others who were themselves stranded on their own islands.

I started the Leading with Heart program confused about leadership and my role. I had accepted that my current role was a management role and would not be a leadership role. I have since learned that, "… leaders and educators must develop themselves but not by themselves" (Ramsden, 1998, p.375). Our cohort met on a sunny July morning with no idea of the journey we were about to embark on together. We met each day for two weeks, and in that time learned to authentically share our personal and professional struggles and triumphs. As I worked through the program, I was pleasantly surprised to discover that the heart-led leadership principles aligned closely to my own values and beliefs. For years I had been trying to fit myself into different leadership ideologies instead of finding what worked *for me*. The frustration and loneliness came not from my inabilities, but rather from a poor fit between myself and different ideologies. Creating a leadership map, personal and professional goals, and a path towards my goals was long overdue. I learned that I could be myself (though arguably a better version) and a leader without compromising on either. I treated my team as I like to be treated: I included them, asked for their opinions before making decisions, and I communicated directly to them news and information that could potentially impact their roles.

From a justice perspective, I learned that being a good leader was as much about caring for myself as it was caring for others. The personal reflection exercises that we went through were not easy, but they were necessary. I reminded myself that I am only human; sometimes certain emotions and feelings may emerge that, as a private person, I would otherwise keep from others. While these emotions exist within my true self, they do not overshadow it. "Although your true nature may be hidden momentarily by stress and worry, anger and unfulfilled longings, it still continues to exist" (Hanson 2009, p. 13). As a leader, I have learned to acknowledge my emotions and to communicate them to my team. Showing others my human side has made it easier for them to relate to me on a personal level. I don't know if I would have had the courage to step away from my preconceived ideas of leadership prior to developing my leadership heart.

To be a leader is to be vulnerable, and to be vulnerable is to feel helpless at times. Like anyone else, I feel vulnerable in certain situations. I struggle in letting others know of my vulnerability. I am grateful to work with people I trust, people I know that I can share with when I need to. When things get tough, I sometimes find myself retreating to my island: old habits are hard to break. When this happens, I either draw upon mindfulness exercises and/or reach out to my Leading with Heart peers for support. I am only alone on my island now if I choose to be.

Finding Resilience

"On your best day, how do you show up?" (Tabrizi & Terrell, 2015, p. 83). For a time, I was not showing up effectively as a leader. The stress was starting to take a physical toll on me. I wanted to do well, but I needed guidance and direction. I had come to accept that I could start the journey by looking for it within myself. Turning to others can be helpful, but there is also a time to be alone with and learn from one's inner wisdom and resources. The first step on my journey towards this heart-led leadership practice was finding ways to show care towards myself.

I first discovered Lawrence's (2018) book entitled, *Your Oxygen Mask First* while browsing online. It ended up being incredibly complimentary to the readings in the Leading with Heart program, especially Hanson (2018). Lawrence (2018) writes of creating resilience rituals, and Hanson (2018) speaks of the importance of finding a personal refuge. A refuge can take many forms, be it a person, place, thing, or activity. "A refuge is anything that protects, nurtures, or uplifts you" (Hanson, 2018, p. 29). This really resonated with me. While I was alone on my island, I had no refuge to keep my stressors at bay. As someone who is generally considered to be an introvert, making the time to recharge is extra important for me. Lawrence (2018) suggests that we need to establish daily habits that help us build our resiliency. Unknowingly, I had created my own resilience ritual out of necessity: at the end of the day, I made a cup of coffee or tea, sat on the couch, watched a television show, and worked on a craft project. Between parenting, working full time, day-to-day adulting, and my studies, this short period of time each day indeed became a refuge. Even today, it doesn't matter what time I get home; this ritual always ends my day.

My friends often marvel at me and ask where I find the time to make crafts with everything that I have going on. What they do not understand is that they too likely have a ritual; it's just that for them it manifests differently. A friend of mine has a dishwasher that broke several years ago. At the time she did not have the money to replace it. Today, years later, she will tell anyone how she does not miss the machine and loves washing her dishes by hand. While washing dishes for me is a special form of punishment, for her it is calming and is one of her resilience rituals.

Previously, I would never have read Lawrence's (2018) book without skipping over any worksheets or parts that asked for reflection. However, I took the time to read and put into practice some of the suggested exercises. I began to give myself the time I deserved for self-care. Now I am aware enough to understand when I need to stop, step back, and put into action the things that ensure self-care. I know when I need a break, and I will act accordingly. What I gained from this program is the ability to recognize the build up of stress sooner, before it manifests into physical symptoms such as irritability, sleep disruptions, muscle tension, and migraine headaches.

Embracing Mindfulness

When first introduced to the concept of mindfulness, my understanding was that to be mindful one had to pause and consider each morsel of food before eating. I could not see the value in that. This led me to have a somewhat jaded view of mindfulness. Later, a professor encouraged me to read the book entitled, "Mindfulness" by Ellen Langer (1989). Langer's practical description and research into mindfulness fascinated me. I read the book cover to cover. The key piece that finally helped me to understand the importance of mindfulness was the description of its opposite meaning: mindlessness. I could relate to many examples in my life where I have acted mindlessly (e.g. arriving at my destination without paying attention to how I got there). Something about the term mindlessness helped it all click into place. If I could act mindlessly, surely, I could start to act mindfully.

I will not say that I act in a mindful way in every facet of my life, but when I find myself getting frustrated or anxious, I know that I need to pause, take several deep breaths, and reflect on why I am feeling this way. It is so easy to fall into old patterns and into mindlessness. To me, working mindfully means purposefully. There have been days when I have been so *busy* trying to clear my inbox, that I have neglected the *people*. Working in a business setting, too often the focus is on *productivity*, meaning that the human side of business can easily be forgotten.

Learning to practice mindfulness with a cohort of emerging leaders was also a helpful experience. Haber-Curran, Allen, & Shankman (2015) remind us that leadership is not an independent exercise. Leadership is social and interpersonal. Mindfulness is also social and interpersonal. This is likely why I struggled in my first few years, as I felt I was alone in the process. Knowing that I can reach out to my cohort for support, and they will respond when I need it, is a comfort that I did not have before. I know that I do not have to follow my path alone unless I want to. When I start to feel overwhelmed and overburdened, I try to remember the wisdom from Michelle Stowe's (2017) Ted Talk, where she said, "calm people practice two things before they respond: breathe and ask questions" (3:12). Before the support of my group, I would have borne the stress and not practiced the self-care that I need. They help me to stay grounded and remind me of the importance of staying in the present.

Helping Others

Since becoming a heart-led leader, I have noticed that I am more aware of others and their own self-awareness. This is similar to Bunting's (2016) realization that, "An accidental benefit of mindfulness for me has been deep insight and intuition into other people, a sensitivity to how people are feeling and what may be causing it" (p. 142). Those who present with less self-awareness especially stand out to me. This is most noticeable in how they react when something goes wrong. My department hosts several events each year, and sometimes things do not always run smoothly. When problems occur, my philosophy is to fix the issue as it arises so as not to impact the event. After the event, there is opportunity to review what happened and create processes to prevent the problem from happening again. Unfortunately for some, their first reaction is to immediately lay blame and deflect attention away from themselves. Bunting (2016) calls this "defensive blaming" (p. 102), and he believes it to be toxic. Previously, these types of reactions would have annoyed me, and I may have reacted negatively. However, I now take note of what the person is telling me, and I respond with, "How does that solve our problem? Let's find a solution now, and we can talk about it later." This strategy has worked well, and over time I have noticed fewer instances of laying blame and more instances of stepping up and taking ownership for difficulties as they arise. I have come to realize that when people know that they will not be reprimanded for an honest mistake, they are less afraid to come forward. "If a manager can risk deviation from routine ways of doing things, creative employees can thrive and contribute" (Langer, 1989, p.136–137). Thus, I try to find ways to direct employees to contribute towards problem-solving instead of being stuck in a mindset of fear and blame.

I recognize the incredible benefits that have come from working on my personal growth and leadership, and also from working within a team; I often wonder what steps I need to take to help others do the same. Is it up to me to point them towards a path, or is it something that they must discover on their own? Do I have to let them fall so they understand the consequences, or will the same lesson be learned if I prevent the fall and simply talk about the danger? As a leader, I believe it is my role to help bring my team members to the point where they outgrow their roles and follow their own path. If I clearly outline my goals and expectations early on, and offer encouragement, recognition, and redirection as needed, eventually there will come a time when they are ready to move on, and as a leader I should be (and I am) proud of their achievements.

Final Thoughts

Where does this leave me now? Did I become the leader that I wanted to, or am I still the manager that I feel I am expected to be? Truthfully, I am a little of both. There are operational requirements where I need to be a manager, but I have approached the role in a new way. Being the manager does not mean that I must be heavy-handed and impersonal. I much prefer being open and honest while communicating as much information as I can to my team. This allows them to understand why decisions are made, and where they fit into the organization. It prevents rumours from circulating.

Like most people, I am a work in progress. I know that I will still make mistakes. Where I once viewed *leadership* as a trendy buzz word used to sell books and courses, now I know the true value that a good leader adds. I also understand that leaders are not necessarily born, they can be made too. Finding the time to focus on the tasks that make me a better person and leader is still a challenge. It can be too easy to fall into old patterns. However, I have been able to make progress through small steps. I bought a journal and regularly record the things that I am grateful for. I make a conscious effort to show gratitude to my team and make time to write out appreciation cards for the contributions of individual team members.

Self-reflection is not easy, but it brings great rewards. I strive to devote time each day for meditation, mindfulness, gratitude, and journaling, but adapting them into my daily life is not yet consistent. The hard work in becoming a heart-led leader is the work that I do on myself. I sometimes find myself slipping into old patterns, but I also recognize when I am doing so. I pause, take a few breaths, simply acknowledge that this is not who I want to be, and move on.

Essentially, I have learned how to look *at* myself and look *after* myself as a leader. It helps to identify what I do well, where I need to grow, and what I need to change. The real desire to be a good leader comes from within, not forcefully outside oneself, and this what inspires sincere change. I have set myself on a solid path that includes the heart and I accept that there will be mistakes made along the way. However, self-forgiveness is required—always. I am grateful. Most importantly, I no longer feel alone on my island. I have a mindful community that is willing to support me on this journey whenever I need it.

References

Avolio, B. J., & Gardner, W. L. (2005). Authentic leadership development: Getting to the root of positive forms of leadership. *The Leadership Quarterly, 16*(3), 315–338. doi: 10.1016/j.leaqua.2005.03.001

Bunting, M. (2016). *The mindful leader: 7 practices for transforming your leadership, your organisation and your life*. Milton: John Wiley & Sons, Incorporated.

Haber-Curran, P., Allen, S., & Shankman, M. (2015). Valuing human significance: Connecting leadership development to personal competence, social competence, and caring. *New Directions for Student Leadership, 2015*(145), 59–70. doi: https://doi-org.ezproxy.lib.ucalgary.ca/10.1002/yd.20124

Hanson, R. (2018). *Resilient: How to grow an unshakable core of calm, strength, and happiness*. New York, NY: Harmony Books

Hanson, R. (2009). *Buddha's brain: The practical neuroscience of happiness, love, & wisdom*. Oakland, CA: New Harbinger.

Langer, E. (1989). *Mindfulness*. Reading, Mass.: Addison-Wesley.

Lawrence, K. (2017). *Your Oxygen Mask First*. USA. Lioncrest Publishing.

Powell, Elizabeth A. (2009). *Writing to reflect: Mindful leadership in the face of change*. Darden Case No. UVA-BC-0217.

Spears, L. C. (2005). The understanding and practice of servant-leadership. *The International Journal of Servant-Leadership, 1*(1), 29–45. Retrieved from http://ezproxy.lib.ucalgary.ca/login?url=https://search.proquest.com/docview/2221125245?accountid=9838

Stowe, M. (2017, October). *Empathy: the heart of difficult conversation* [video]. TEDxTallaght. https://www.ted.com/talks/michelle_stowe_empathy_the_heart_of_difficult_conversations?language=en

Tabrizi, B., & Terrell, M. (2015). The inside-out effect: A practical guide to transformational leadership. Ashland, OH: Evolve Publishing.

Wermuth-Buffer, M. (December 2018). *Why being a manager is a career change, not a promotion*. Retrieved from: https://www.fastcompany.com/90282088/why-being-a-manager-is-a-career-change-not-a-promotion#new_tab

Wheatley, M. (2002). Turning to one another: Simple conversations to restore hope to the future. *The Journal for Quality and Participation, 25*(2), 8–19. Retrieved from http://ezproxy.lib.ucalgary.ca/login?url=https://search-proquest-com.ezproxy.lib.ucalgary.ca/docview/219134227?accountid=9838

Chapter 5

One Breath at a Time

Lisa Talbot

"Listen. Are you breathing just a little and calling it a life?"
(Mary Oliver, 1997)

Inhale — exhale — repeat. Breathing is a life-sustaining process that has the power to bring peace in the present moment (Brown & Olson, 2015; Patel, 2014). It is essential for alignment between the self, environment, and community. Breathing is also the first step in balancing our physical and mental states. By engaging in several cycles of deep inhalation followed by exhalation, physiological responses slow; one pauses, and responds to challenging situations with clarity, formulating creative solutions, increased resilience, and an improved ability to balance work and home life (Brown & Olson, 2015). The connection between breathing and state of mind is well documented (Basso et al., 2019; Beblo et al., 2018; Brown & Olson, 2015; Hanson, 2018; Telles & Singh, 2013), and it is a crucial connection for mindful leadership (Brendel & Bennett, 2016). By accessing and utilizing the breath in mindfulness practices, we are empowered to become the greatest expressions of ourselves and in turn empower others to reach their full potential (Brown, Ryan & Creswell, 2007). With the expansion of the lungs comes an expansion of awareness of oneself, which can potentially spread outwards from an individual to an organization.

Ah! It feels great to breathe! This chapter will describe how I learned to appreciate this natural human resource through preparing as a heart-led leader from the inside out. I will address how mindfulness practices, rooted in breath, laid the foundations for the awareness and development of self-care, community care, and justice in my role as an emerging leader. Furthermore, I will describe how tools, such as a Leadership Map and a Manifesto, provided the necessary experiential learning to be a heart-led leader. I advocate building an inventory of mindful practices; this has become part of my foundation, and is the core of my approach when I initiate actions aligned with self and social justice. This process, which contains outcomes, patterns and tensions, will be examined and shared. Arising from my ability to honor and learn from the breath, these gifts nurtured my capacity for self-care and community care as I learned how to breathe life into my developing leadership role. Inhale—exhale—repeat. Breathe.

Breathing Life into Learning Tasks - A Leadership Map

A key exercise in my journey as an emerging leader was the creation of a personalized visual representation of my leadership journey: a leadership map. This map helped me explore how to lead from a place of authenticity, wisdom, and heart. The map included a framework composed of mindfulness practices, integrated with teachings and applications that included the heart, wisdom, vision, and action. Mindfulness applications (such as mindful breathing) were used to help explore and deepen the connections of these resources.

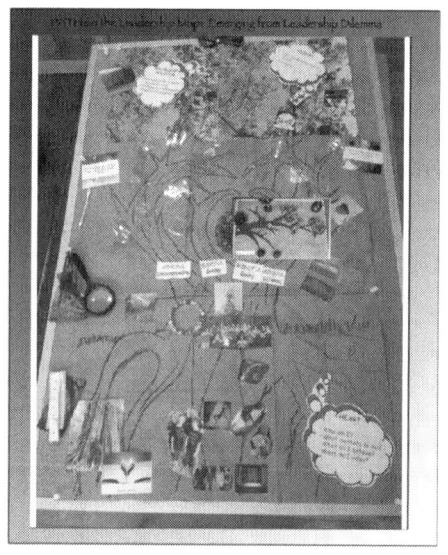

Figure 1. Leadership Map. A visual representation of a leadership journey.

The map was anchored in the symbolic image of a tree, one of the world's great breathers, as well as a key provider of human oxygen. Please refer to Figure 1 below, entitled *Leadership Map*.

As represented on the map, mindful and inspired leadership emerges from the roots of what I consider the heart. This includes knowledge of who I am, my identity, along with my beliefs and values. When a trusted advisor viewed my leadership map, he shared this piece of wisdom from a First Nations Elder: "When the storm comes and you are out in the branches, the place to return to is the trunk" (Anonymous, personal communication, Aug. 19, 2018). For me, the trunk represents the Present Moment, the core of my leadership practice, which is developed through the practice of being present. The trunk is the strongest part of the tree, and in my map it supports a canopy of leaves that metaphorically represent both wisdom and vision. All parts of the tree—roots, trunk, branches, and leaves—engage in an interactive relationship initiating from my core values and personal vision, which have been cultivated by mindful practices. The trunk of the tree reminds me how my own trunk—my human body—contains all the necessary apparatus that allows me to breathe.

When paying attention to the sensation of breath in my body, I receive instant awareness of the precious present moment. Each inhale and exhale of my own trunk includes the wisdom of the heart, giving rise to the powerful way of being that is the foundation of heart-led leadership. In the next section, I will describe how the breath naturally allowed me to grasp the gifts of the present moment, empowering and freeing my leadership strengths and abilities.

Cultivating Awareness of Breath Through Mindfulness Practice

The first step in building a personal mindful practice was an awareness of breath. Brown & Olsen (2015) advocate practicing "breath inquiry," (p. 80); this means you have an awareness of a connection between breath and your state of mind. For example, as I struggle with writing this chapter in the present moment, I inhale and exhale; after becoming more grounded and present, I notice my posture is slumped, each breath is tight and shallow, and I am feeling anxious about deadlines. As the present moment invites further exploration, I notice feelings of tension and guilt as family, work, and writing tasks compete for attention. I am reminded of Brown & Olsen's (2015) idea that sometimes, "behind breath holding there is an intense sense of being overwhelmed" (p. 58). I am aware of the voice of the inner-critic, evaluating each idea as it appears on the page. I align my posture and take another cycle of breath. Inhaling. Exhaling. As I lift my chest and fresh air expands my abdomen, new energy arises. This awareness and acceptance of discomfort in the present moment helps me realize that there is a space between thoughts and feelings, and who I am. I have thoughts, but I am not my thoughts (Kabat-Zinn, 1999, 2007). This tool for self-care has been instrumental for helping me slow down and be in the present moment without self-judgment.

Along with using breath inquiry to support self-care as described above, it was also crucial for helping me practice self-justice. Without actually being aware of it, embarking on the journey towards a master's degree was a critical step in self-justice, one that allowed me to recognize my own potential and move towards actualizing leadership aspirations. Sitting in our circle, on the first morning of a class dedicated to cultivating the heart of leaders, I was flooded with many self-defeating thoughts. The inner-critic questioned my priorities, my abilities, and my place in a graduate-level leadership program. It had been twenty years since my last post-secondary experience, and I felt like an imposter, completely out of my element.

Additionally, during the program's first morning session on campus, my emotions were close to the surface; I felt horrified when I dissolved into tears as we each introduced ourselves and identified our reasons for pursuing heart-led leadership. I later realized that this was actually a moment of vulnerability, opening the way to build relationships and a safe learning place within our group's circle of trust. This process was very different than the norm in my professional context. However, I learned that instead of allowing my emotions to be in control, I could effectively listen, understand, and respond, rather than react. Working with the breath allowed me to work through challenging thoughts and emotions with acceptance and understanding. Thich Nhat Hanh (2016) describes breath as, "the bridge which connects life to consciousness, which unites your body to your thoughts. Whenever your mind becomes scattered, use your breath as the means to take hold of your mind again" (p. 15). Learning to process my thoughts and emotions in a helpful way left more energy to access intuition, creativity, and awareness. Empowered by these strengths, I am better prepared to develop and pursue a clear vision of teaching and leading with authenticity.

Tabrizi (2015) states that, "The greater the amount of emotional weight ascribed to a new activity, the greater the chance that the activity is retained as a habit long term" (p. 167). That which has an emotional connection is more apt to be learned and remembered. For me, this emotionally-laden learning came in the form of a challenge to my physical wellness.

Days after we completed our on-campus portion of a leadership preparation program, I was hospitalized with pneumonia, and mindfulness practice became a life-line. Tools that focused on the breath and learning to be with the present moment were invaluable during my hospital stay and the following six-month recovery period.

During this time, the natural process of breathing through damaged lungs was agonizing. Paired with a harsh summer of forest fires and related air quality issues, a deep and lasting gratitude for the simple, repetitive process of inhaling and exhaling was sparked. Inhale—Exhale—Breathe. This experience forced me to step back, embrace self-care, and prioritize wellness above all else. Awareness and acceptance became vital in being able to recover while returning to my day-to-day responsibilities. I found an inner resilience that was nurtured breath by breath, learning how to nestle deep into the trunk of the self through mindfulness practices, such as paying attention to each breath.

As I struggled with the challenges of recovering from pneumonia and the chaos of a new school year, I was unexpectedly offered a formalized leadership role as acting assistant principal. The experiences with mindfulness and developing the heart, including self-compassion, equipped me with the tools to deal effectively with others and to prioritize personal well-being while stepping into this leadership role. As *acting* assistant principal the voice of the inner critic arose, as did the imposter syndrome. The importance of the adage *fake it till you make it,* took on new meaning (Cuddy, 2008). I was aware of the need to own my power and internalize the confidence in my own abilities. Sandberg (2013) provided timely advice when she addressed the imposter syndrome as it relates to women in leadership. She advises women to recognize those fundamental qualities that make us unique, claim our achievements, quit internalizing failures, and be our authentic selves. This is described as bringing one's full self to the table. Leaning into this process, I was able to act in the spirit of self-justice, building both confidence and competence, and show up with my skills and abilities as a growing leader.

One example of the above is my changed relationship to conflict. I became aware of a pattern of avoiding conflict and learned instead to reframe it, as described by Francis (2018):

"hold tension in life-giving ways ... it's a dynamic, active practice ... think of holding tension as opening the heart and opening the mind so that under tension they don't shatter, they expand ... holding tension is an inner process of owning your emotions" (p.141).

Tabrizi (2015) reminds me that change is only possible once I am deeply self-aware and acknowledge my unique experiences, tensions, and struggles. When considering the depth and breadth of how mindfulness has impacted my life, I agree with Lyddy (2017), who notes that mindfulness "beneficially impacts how individuals function at work" (p. 3). Of particular resonance, an increased ability to respond to emotionally charged situations or confrontations in a calm, present, and non-reactive state (Lyddy, 2017). This non-reactive state acts as a boundary or barrier between events and my emotional response, which has been incredibly liberating. Working as a school administrator can feel like living in a wasp nest. The tree on my leadership map represents this, however, the nest is also surrounded by mindful branches, embracing the shape of a heart. This speaks to the heart-led leadership practices and mindful actions in which to hold the tension of any issue.

The practice of mindfulness, as well as an authentic, intentional vision and mission, rooted in values, allowed me to navigate the complexities of conflicts and dilemmas.

In my new role as assistant principal, I also found mindful breathing an important anchor to guide me through the swarm of the day. It has become a routine to practice mindful breathing every night before bed, and again each morning, as I set a daily intention. Prior to building these practices, my mind would swirl with anxiety, trying to process the happenings of the day and catalogue all of the things left to do. When I would step into the school each morning, often before I even got past the door, I would become immediately engaged in the pressing issues, lacking awareness to practice compassion for self and others. Finding moments in the day to practice both formal and informal mindfulness practices such as stopping, pausing, observing, and breathing (Brown & Olsen, 2015, p. 85), allowed me to focus on what is truly important, and helped me align my actions with my beliefs and act with integrity. However, this also involved more inner work on my part; this is discussed in the next section.

A Leadership Manifesto: Values and Vision

Just as a tree requires sunlight and the surface area of leaves to complete the process of providing oxygen, mindful reflection is required when accessing inner wisdom, uncovering values, and developing vision. This awareness centers on the breath.

The development of a Leadership Manifesto allowed me to examine and articulate fundamental beliefs and core values to form a guiding vision. I defined and reflected upon how my beliefs, values, gifts, and strengths contribute to my effectiveness as a leader. These beliefs and values center around the heart of leadership. As the heart circulates blood to the lungs to become oxygenated, the values, beliefs, and strengths impact leading, learning, resourcing, and sustaining leadership initiatives. The work of articulating core values and developing a calling vision statement (Tabrizi, 2013) is deeply reflective and requires time. Engaging simultaneously in course work and a formal leadership role, I wondered how I would be able to undertake this work. However, I found that having a mindfulness practice helped me to combat the "allostatic load and the negativity bias" that can drain me and eliminates my ability to be self-aware (Bunting, 2016, p. 2).

In learning how to identify my values, along with my passion, spark, or birthright gifts, I also took the time to look at what might be blocking some of these from showing up fully in my life and work. Growing up in a family where the disease of addiction was present throughout much of my childhood, I become adept at the art of peace-making, conflict avoidance, care-taking, and people pleasing, often sacrificing my truth in the process. This survival mechanism evolved into a need to mask feelings of insecurity through perfectionism, and through my adolescence, right into my early twenties, translated into self-neglect. There was an ever-present void of feeling not good enough and not belonging, which led to a number of unhelpful coping behaviors. Throughout my early teen years, I excelled academically and was an outspoken advocate for peers, especially the disenfranchised. In high school, tired of feeling ostracized, I succumbed to the pressure to conform, with the stark realization that in order to fit in I needed to silence my opinions. I lost the ability to speak my truth, and after the tenth grade I do not recall voluntarily speaking in class, preferring to be invisible. This persisted throughout my undergraduate degree and early stages as a teacher.

Twenty years later, as I explored contemplative practices such as mindful breathing, I had the opportunity to create a space within my body, mind, and heart to delve into my spark and reconnect with what makes me feel most alive. This includes speaking in public, being a knowledge seeker, and having a love of learning. From this awareness I was able to reclaim my voice. A recognition of patterns and tensions of the past allowed me to recognize negative self-talk and self-defeating actions. I found the courage to speak from a place of awareness and authenticity.

Community Care and Justice

Presently, community care and justice primarily emerge from the way in which I approach interactions. Cultivating a collection of mindful practices has given me the awareness to meet others with understanding and has allowed me to experience more empathy. For example, during highly confrontational experiences with students, parents, or other staff members, the practice of mindful listening has resulted in me seeking to understand before being understood. The energy of listening flows over into understanding: "The deep listening without judgment is what really opens your heart to people who are different than you" (Francis, 2018, p. 139). Hearing a story from the perspective of the *other* and asking questions to understand the *why* behind actions has helped to diffuse highly volatile situations. An examination of my own biases, and those that may be institutionally ingrained, has allowed for the movement beyond awareness into socially-just actions.

One example related to the above stands out: it took place when a teacher stormed into the office, frustrated and demanding support to deal with a defiant and disruptive student. My personal experience echoed the relentless challenges of day-to-day teaching, and with the intent to fully support staff I asked the teacher how she would like to see the problem solved—and then proceeded to follow her suggestions. While I should have attended to the subtle, persistent feeling that my actions were not in alignment with what I believed, I also wanted to show that I was a supportive administrator. There was a tension between my belief in the importance of building relational trust with the teacher and hearing the voice of the student to understand their unique learning needs. The teacher had wanted me to have the student write a letter to his parents explaining his behaviour, and after following through with this, the next day I was met with a furious, accusatory email from the student's parent, complete with personal attacks, notably copied directly to my principal. My instinctive reaction was defensive and self-justifying as I dashed off a response, wanting the parent to see the school's side of the story. However, before hitting the send button, I stepped back from the situation, became aware of my reaction, and intentionally took a mindful pause. As difficult as it was in the moment, I realized there was something deeper at play that required compassion. We decided to hold a meeting with the parents, and it became clear that we were not addressing the needs of the student who had significant social-emotional and learning complexities. Both the student and his parents were entitled to a voice in the process and agency in how these situations would be approached in the future. Mindful listening on the part of the leadership team was critical. Meeting with all stakeholders with the intent to hear the wisdom of the inner-voice of others allowed for a collaborative solution, in the spirit of community care, to be reached. In the process, the student/parent-school relationship was strengthened.

Community care also involved others sharing their mindful practices, something I have approached with reluctance, knowing that research demonstrates "teachers must develop their own practice of mindfulness so that they can provide the scaffolding and modeling that is essential for helping students flourish in their own development of mindfulness skills" (Eva & Thayer, 2017, p. 21). Currently, I am taking small steps to expand my mindful practices and share them with others. This includes speaking about my experiences at educational conferences, presenting to students new to leadership programs, and writing for an expanded audience. These activities relate to self-justice in that they give voice to and validate my personal experience, and the value in sharing this with others.

Following the Dream: Breath by Breath

I am filled with gratitude for the gifts provided through the experiential learning in a graduate leadership program. Mindfulness and contemplative practices helped shape my vision, which is represented on my leadership map in the image of a tree—an oxygen generator—without which, I would be unable to find my breath. As I focus on the breath, I remember my core values and beliefs, and I am growing in my capacity to apply them daily. The breath helps to serve the process of self-justice and social justice as I work towards empowering myself and others, one breath at a time. Elizabeth Gilbert (2016) discusses "the natural order of life: the eternal inhale and exhale of action and reaction" (p. 124). Through the process of breathing with heart I am able to initiate the process of leading with heart. Inhale—exhale—repeat.

References

Basso, J. C., McHale, A., Ende, V., Oberlin, D. J., & Suzuki, W. A. (2019). Brief, daily meditation enhances attention, memory, mood, and emotional regulation in non-experienced meditators. *Behavioural Brain Research, 1*(356), p. 208–220. Available from University of Calgary Database. https://www-sciencedirect-com.ezproxy.lib.ucalgary.ca/science/article/pii/S016643281830322X

Beblo, T., Pelster, S., Schilling, C., Kleinke, K., Iffland, B., Driessen, M., Fernando, S. (2018).

Breath versus emotions: The impact of different foci of attention during mindfulness meditation on the experience of negative and positive emotions. *Behavior Therapy, 49*(5), p. 702–714. Available from University of Calgary Database. https://www-sciencedirect-com.ezproxy.lib.ucalgary.ca/science/article/pii/S0005789417301363

Brendel, W., & Bennett, C. (2016). Learning to embody leadership through mindfulness and somatics practice. *Advances in Developing Human Resources, 18*(3), p. 409–425. Available from University of Calgary Database. https://journals-sagepub-com.ezproxy.lib.ucalgary.ca/doi/abs/10.1177/1523422316646068

Brown, V., & Olson, K. (2015). *The mindful school leader: Practices to transform your leadership and your school*. London, UK: Corwin Press.

Brown, K., Ryan, R., & Creswell, J. (2007). Mindfulness: Theoretical Foundations and Evidence for its Salutary Effects. *Psychological Inquiry, 18*(4), 211–237. Retrieved February 8, 2020, from www.jstor.org/stable/20447389

Bunting, M. (2016). *The mindful leader: 7 practices for transforming your leadership, your organization and your life*. Available online from University of Calgary Database. http://ebookcentral.proquest.com.ezproxy.lib.ucalgary.ca/lib/ucalgary-ebooks/detail.action?docID=4516137

Center for Courage & Renewal & Francis, S. L. (2018). *The courage way: Leading and living with integrity* [E-book]. Oakland, CA: Berrett-Koehler.

Cuddy, A. (2012). Fake it till you make it [Video file]. *TEDTalk*. Retrieved from https://www.youtube.com/watch?v=RVmMeMcGc0Y

Gilbert, E. (2016). *Big magic*. Penguin USA. Eva, A. & Thayer, N. (2017) The Mindful Teacher: Translating Research into Daily Well-being, *The Clearing House: A Journal of Educational Strategies, Issues and Ideas, 90*:1, 18–25, DOI: 10.1080/00098655.2016.1235953

Hạnh Nhất, T. & Ho, M. (2016). *The miracle of mindfulness: an introduction to the practice of meditation*. Boston: Beacon Press.

Hanson, R. (2018). Resilient: How to grow an unshakable core of calm, strength, and happiness. New York, NY: Harmony Books.

Kabat-Zinn, J. (1999). Indra's net at work: The mainstreaming of Dharma practice in society. In G. Watson, S. Batchelor, & G. Claxton (Eds.), *The psychology of awakening: Buddhism, science, and our day-to-day lives*. London: Rider.

Kabat-Zinn, J. (2007). Mindfulness with Jon Kabat-Zinn [Video file]. Retrieved from https://www.youtube.com/watch?v=3nwwKbM_vJc&t=9s

Lyddy, C. J., & Good, D. G. (2017). Being while doing: An inductive model of mindfulness at work. *Frontiers in Psychology, 7*, pp. 1–18. Retrieved from: https://www.ncbi.nlm.nih.gov/pmc/articles/PMC5318448/pdf/fpsyg-07-02060.pdf

Sandberg, S., (2014). *Facebook COO Sheryl Sandberg Commencement Speech Harvard Commencement 2014* [Video file]. Retrieved from: https://www.youtube.com/watch?v=ZKII4AwLKkU

Tabrizi, B., & Terrell, M. (2015). *The inside-out effect: A practical guide to transformational leadership*. Ashland, OH: Evolve Publishing.

Telles, S., & Singh, N. (2013). Science of the Mind. *Psychiatric Clinics of North America, 36*(1), 93–108.

Chapter Six

The Sounds of Silence

Katie McIntyre

Silence ... I'm going to just let that word hang there for a minute, to give you a chance to get comfortable with it.

If we were talking face-to-face, and I left that silent space there, one or both of us might jump in to fill the void. You might wonder about the reasons for my silence. Am I uncomfortable? Maybe I simply forgot what I was going to say? You might feel nervous, or even embarrassed for what some might consider a social faux-pas. What is it about silence that makes so many of us uncomfortable? More importantly, how can we shift our personal experiences with silence to embrace its benefits? By exploring our perceptions of silence and learning how to be comfortable in the space it provides, this chapter aims to illustrate the importance of this essential tool in preparing for leadership, and cultivating self-compassion.

Befriending Silence

What is silence? It is many things. It is the air that hangs in a conversation between sentences. It is the first moments of the day before anyone else in the house wakes up. Silence may be the absence of intentional sound. Quiet ... on purpose. No playlists, no Netflix, no witty banter. And for many, it causes intense discomfort. We leap into conversations to fill the emptiness. We use earbuds, home stereos, and car radios to ensure a constant soundtrack in our lives. Many people avoid it at all costs, and in the process drown out the beauty that silence holds, missing opportunities for learning and growth. As silence advocate Parker Palmer describes:

> "The impact of silence is not only solace, but disturbance. Silence forces you to look at your life in some very challenging ways. I think in our culture that's one of the reasons silence is not popular. It's one of the reasons we fill the air with noise ... our minds with noise, because we avoid having to take that deep dive into ourselves" (Hall, Johnson, & McColman, 2018, 8:20).

I have an evolving relationship with silence. For example, on the first day of our Leading with Heart program, I learned an invaluable lesson. Our instructor provided us with a poem and invited students to read parts of it aloud in our new circle. Whoever felt so inclined to go first could start. Silence hung in the air. My mind was racing in my discomfort. I've sat in many professional development sessions where no one is willing to be vulnerable or brave, and my instinct was to jump in and get the reading over with, to move the day along. I was also vibrating with nerves, this being my first day of university in well over a decade, and perhaps suffering from a mild case of imposter syndrome—who did I think I was sitting in this circle with these intelligent and talented people?

I waited about 1.2 seconds before I dove in and became the first reader—not because I *wanted* to, but because I needed to fill the deafening silence. I was *so* uncomfortable sitting in a room with nineteen other humans with no noise to fill the space. The sound of people breathing. The shuffling of feet and papers, laced with obvious discomfort. Feeling torn, and not wanting to read aloud to the group, but also not enjoying the quiet moment; it was incredibly overwhelming for me given that I am someone who generally avoids silence at all costs. On the second day of class, we welcomed an empty chair to our circle: a seat for silence. This chair was a physical reminder that silence was always allowed a place in the circle, a reminder to breathe, settle into each moment, to take a pause before responding. I turned a corner in my relationship with silence that day. Instead of foe, I saw a friend, who gently reminds me to relax, reflect, and at times, just *be*.

These lessons with silence continued throughout the days ahead. During our first group mindfulness practice I was still overwhelmed with discomfort. I most certainly was not in the present moment, focusing on my breathing. I was aware, however, of a tightening in my chest, a desire to shift my body, and maybe to run out of the room and not look back. The discomfort was so great that I almost started to laugh. (You know, that awkward laughter that comes when you are accused of doing something you didn't do, but somehow makes you look one thousand percent guilty?) Previously, my only experience with mindfulness practice was by myself, in the privacy of my home. Twenty people sitting together in silence? No thank you!

However, although I thought this experience was certainly *not* for me, I have learned time and time again that this experience was *indeed for* me. I learned that silence is powerful. Silence is healing. Discomfort is okay. Embracing silence has given me the space to connect with my mindfulness practice in new ways. I now live with more intention and gratitude. I am able to turn to silence during times of anxiety and overstimulation to calm my mind and focus on the present moment.

As the days on campus passed, my comfort in that circle expanded exponentially. By the end, we sat together comfortably, in silence, for up to half an hour. Those quiet minutes in a room filled with people who were no longer strangers are some of the moments I most cherish in my journey to embrace silence.

Silence and Leadership

Welcoming silence into my heart, and my life, has allowed me to be a better communicator, teacher, and leader. The chance to reflect and just *be* is intimidating and uncomfortable at first. "Having plenty of stimuli makes it easy for us to distract ourselves from what we're feeling. But when there is silence, all these things present themselves clearly" (Nhat Hanh, 2015, p. 24). It has taken me decades to let go of the distractions and embrace quiet in my life. Even as a recovering silence avoider, I sometimes relapse and require a jazzy playlist quietly crooning from my laptop speaker in order to get anything done. Recovering the essence of silence is a slow journey. In a world full of distractions, author Jane Brox (2019) reminds us that "as contemporary life pushes silence to the corners, a longing for it persists, as does faith that it offers something the noise of the world cannot provide" (p. 245).

For me, silence is the greatest gift I've ever received. It has provided me with many things, such as the ability to support my mental health, be present for others, and share the benefits of silence with the people around me. For example, sitting in silence has helped me feel calmer and provided clarity when thinking over challenges, or just helped me de-stress from the busyness and noise of the day. Bernardi, Porta, and Sleight (2006) have shown how silence can lower the heart-rate and relax the mind and body. Additionally, silence can help replenish our mental resources, particularly attentional resources that are critical for being present in demanding circumstances such as what leaders encounter (Kaplan, 1995).

The benefit of silence has had an important role in my interactions with others. As an emerging leader, I practice using silence effectively when I am working with my colleagues. A moment of silence carefully placed in a conversation shows patience, offers a space for contributions from others, and helps to powerfully reinforce my ideas. Without silence, I am not afforded the opportunity to listen deeply. Being engaged in dialogue with others and allowing moments of silence may be the difference between genuine connection and surface conversation. Leaving room to breathe between words provides space for everyone to think, reflect, and respond mindfully. The inclination to interrupt is more evidence that we avoid silence as often as possible. Instead of listening to understand, we are listening to respond. Scott Miller, author and thought leader, suggests closing your mouth and counting to seven in your head to counteract interrupting (Hollis, 2019, 31:10). Using silence to provide space for others is a sign of authentic communication and generosity. The gift of quiet can be used for deep reflection and an opportunity to "break the cycle of busyness in our lives" (Becker, n.d., para. 13).

It is important to note that the move towards *silent leadership* does not equate to meek or passive qualities. Instead, "silent leaders are compassionate, understanding, open and approachable and–most importantly–they command their team through earned respect rather than force of character" (Petch, 2016, para 7). Leaders who embody this skill do not lack in direction or strength. Quite the opposite. They must be good listeners who lead by example and offer empathy to their teams in order to build trust (Petch, 2016).

The value of silence is powerful, a subtle but influential leadership tool. In team meetings, I often use silence to hold space for people as they reflect and express their feelings and opinions. By offering quiet pauses in conversation, I provide colleagues the opportunity to hear who they are, what they need, and how to effectively get where they need to go. Silence winds up being the "tool to help [them] find their own tools" (Bourg Carter, 2013, para. 4). I provide colleagues with a safe space and a listening ear, which is often what they want, and more so, what they need. Instead of offering a solution, I provide quiet.

In a recent conversation with a colleague, my practice with silence was put to the test. They came to me seeking advice to navigate relationship tensions they were experiencing with another member of our work community. I could have jumped in, commiserated, and connected their story to my own experience. Instead, I took a deep breath and left a silent pause in the conversation. Given the space to think, my friend continued to explain more of the situation, shared how it was making them feel, and made a connection back to their personal perspective compared to that of the third party. By the end of the conversation, I had done little but listen intently. However, my friend found their way to a pleasing solution for both people involved, and did so in a way that left them feeling empowered and heard.

I also enjoy tuning into others' joys and struggles in a way that would not be possible if every void was filled with only my perspective and voice. Silence is more than a space-filler: it is an intentional leadership strategy designed to involve others in the process of decision-making and vision-casting for the future. "Today's leaders need strong listening skills as power is shared, decision-making is mutual and ideas are melded into a coherent ideology of the future to which all can contribute" (Condon & Hegge, 2014, p. 112). By creating a community-based strategy for problem-solving, the isolation often related to self-care is reduced. Rather than bombarding someone with opinions, or worse, leaving them to deal with their problems by themselves, I strive to offer a safe space for reflection and open dialogue. I try to ask questions to help them come to the heart of their issues, but in choosing silence as a response I can focus more on listening than telling people what to do.

Our most important role as leaders is to raise up those around us. Using mindful compassion (Bunting, 2016) to see the struggles of others creates deeper, more meaningful connections. To be a strong leader is to lead with a generous heart and believe the best of our team members. "We help brighten their light by first *seeing* their light – even perhaps especially, if they can't see it themselves" (p. 116).

Leading with Silence in the Classroom

After my initial rumblings with silence in the first two courses in the Leading with Heart program, I returned to my grade one-two classroom, eager to introduce my new friend Silence to my twenty-four first and second grade students. Many of these children had limited opportunities to experience intentional silence in their lives, and I wanted to use silence as a way to promote health and wellness. Mindfulness practices that involve silence are helpful tools for assisting young students to develop self-awareness, deal with stress, and gain better control of negative thoughts and emotions (Weare, 2018).

The first days (weeks!) were tough. My students' discomfort paralleled mine, and, at times, I thought that I was crazy for trying to introduce the practice of mindful silence in this way. Incorporating silence within mindfulness requires practice, and much like my first days in the Leading with Heart circle, my students struggled through even the briefest moments of quiet. They whispered to each other. They blurted out questions as they popped into their minds. They fidgeted and got up to get drinks of water. Through mindfulness games and activities where we activated our five senses and learned to focus on our breathing, they went from twenty-four unsettled, wiggly bodies to a circle of calm, quiet, and engaged children.

As the months passed, I noticed that the students were better able to come into the classroom in the morning, sit down in our circle, and just *be*. They hung up their coats, changed their shoes, and took their places with little direction from me. Some would close their eyes. They were still and calm and quiet. Sometimes I provided a guided breathing meditation for them, and sometimes we just sat. In modeling my well-practiced ability to sit somewhat comfortably in silence, they began to embrace it too. Throughout our day, I embedded contemplative practices: ". . . anything that brings students into present moment awareness. This state of awareness might come through art, music, or walks in nature" (Wall, 2014, p. 137). Through stories, play, and conversations, I encouraged my students to use the mindfulness activities that we did in the classroom any time they needed them. We talked openly about emotions, and how the tools we used in the classroom could help us work through both positive and negative feelings in a healthy way.

The next year, the transition was far quicker. I had grown more comfortable with the absence of noise, and Silence and I were even better friends. Within a few days, the students in my new group could sit quietly for several minutes. Fortunately, half of our circle was already prepared to sit and be comfortable with silence; half of my class was with me from the previous year, so I had twelve miniature models of quiet contemplation. The grade one students looked to the grade two students as role models, allowing them to set the tone in the unfamiliar classroom. The second-grade students took their places in the circle and gently guided our new friends to join us. Smiles and a quiet finger on their lips was all it took to impart the need for quiet and calm. It took less than a week for them to embrace the quiet, peaceful circle, and help the new members of the class to embrace silence as well.

Not only do students reap the benefits of embracing silence, but I also recognize notable changes in myself. These quiet moments, in community with my students, allow me to connect with a smile or welcoming eye contact. It provides us time to be present in the space, and take a few deep breaths before we dive into the learning ahead each day. On the rare day where I have gotten stuck in a snowstorm-induced traffic jam and arrived at school late, and thus missed this opportunity to bask in our silent circle, I feel a constant weight on me through the remainder of the day. My focus is poor, my breathing is shallow, and my mind races in circles. I rely on those moments of silence as much as my students seem to.

I took my practice of mindfulness and silence beyond my students to include other staff members as well. Hosting a weekly meditation in my classroom has allowed other teachers to develop this powerful skill, and created a small community of people with whom I share resources and ideas to cultivate mindfulness and use silence as a tool. In the future, I plan to continue this meditative practice group, with the hope of extending it to more staff. Beyond the group meditation, I also plan to send weekly mindfulness emails with simple strategies to implement mindfulness in classrooms, and beyond the walls of the school.

Diving into the Silent Depths: Finding Self-Compassion

The practice of welcoming silence is not easy. For me, I have learned to better manage and navigate the ebb and flow between comfort and discomfort. However, I notice silence is now more present in all aspects of my life. When I drive, I often turn the radio off, just to enjoy the quiet. While working on the computer, I often choose to do so without music or TV on in the background. I am now able to fall asleep without The Office playing quietly from my phone. As someone who has struggled with an anxiety disorder for the better part of my adult life, I am grateful for the comfort that silence now offers. When the world is overwhelming, instead of filling the quiet with noise to drown out my feelings of unrest, I now sit in the silence. I explore my thoughts, emotions, and triggers without judgment, giving myself the care and nurturing my inner life requires. I recognize when sensory overload is causing harm, and I intentionally seek silence in my day as a form of self-care: filling my cup with silence, a safe space where I can breathe, refocus, and find gratitude, helps sustain me.

If you have been reading and nodding, checking off your own list of reasons why silence brings you discomfort, and noting the strategies you use to avoid it, then know you are in good company. However, also know that you don't have to live in fear of silence. You can, with surprisingly minimal effort and resources, learn to embrace silence as a tool in your work as an educator and leader. Mindfulness can help open the door to silence. Mindfulness allows one to be present and actively aware of one's thoughts, to explore dreams and desires, and to know yourself and what makes you who you truly are. By quieting the external world, we can tune in more attentively to the inner voice and get to know our most authentic selves.

I can now acknowledge my current state of being and accept it without trying to change it. If I am feeling anxious, rather than resisting that feeling, I take a few moments of silence to consider what I am experiencing, and then ground myself in the current moment. The time that silence allows for reflection has helped me identify my strength as a leader and my passion for growth and development. It is in the silence that I set goals, make plans to achieve them, and hone my communication skills by considering both my intentions and my words *before* I say them.

Wall (2014) notes the value of mindfulness meditation and its benefits of "improved academic achievement, enhanced self-acceptance, improved self-care, and overall stress reduction" (p. 138). I am now able to identify my anxiety triggers and calm myself more quickly than in the past. My focus, productivity, and general well-being have improved exponentially. I am better able to communicate my needs and take steps to meet them. Through this practice I am also more observant and aware of the needs of others. Through the practice of mindfulness and opening myself up to embrace silence, I am growing in my ability to be self-aware, which impacts "other-awareness," an important skill for effective leadership (Bunting, 2016).

I invite you to take a minute and explore silence. Close your eyes and tune in to your breath. Where do you feel your breath in your body at this moment? Notice the sensations of breath at your nostrils, your chest, or your belly. Inhale—Exhale—Inhale—Exhale ... Then notice how you feel in this moment. Notice both comfort and discomfort. Allow silence to create a space around these feelings. Just notice. Within the stillness, you may observe sounds, like the ticking of the clock, the quiet hum of the fridge, the cat lapping at the water dish. Sounds such as these arise out of the present moment and the silence, and they are reminders of the things that I am grateful for: the peaceful morning hours I claim for myself, the coziness of the winter season, the beautiful family whom I adore more than anything. Silence is a paradigm that holds discomfort and comfort in the form of gratitude.

Appreciating silence can be cultivated through active choices, both in your own home and in other spaces too. Try turning the music off in the car. Last week, the podcast I was listening to on my drive to work had ended, and I paused it. I could then hear the buzz of the stereo, so I turned that off too. Then I noticed the sound of the heater; it was loud, but because it was a cold morning, I left it on. I spent the rest of my commute in silence, or as near to silence as you can get when navigating city streets during rush hour. After the initial anxiety of quiet wore off, I settled into the peace of silence, listening only to my own thinking. I don't know that I thought about anything earth-shattering; what I do know is simply that when I intentionally practice listening to the sounds of silence, I feel more centered, focused, and ready to start the day.

Conclusion

I am grateful to have been reacquainted with silence during the Leading with Heart program. Silence is meant to be welcomed. The silence that we learned to embrace in our circle was where some of my most in-depth learning took place. I learned to slow down and reflect, rather than speaking without thinking. When we came together in our circle I was afraid, and I am sure I was not the only one. I learned how to be open to the spaces within myself, and between others, that silence provides. I learned how to be more comfortable sitting in a circle of twenty not-strangers being incredibly present in my body and the space of that room, which has helped me become more open, inviting, and comfortable in the spaces that I occupy as a leader, as a friend, as a human being.

Most importantly, befriending silence has created an opportunity to listen to my heart. This journey has acquainted me with the fierce woman quietly waiting inside, with potential that could only be unlocked within the silence. Through my experiences with silence, I feel like I know myself better, and that I have developed many important skills that are essential for leaders, such as finding calm in the storm, using silence to invite others to a conversation with their inner selves, and deeply enjoying the present moment and the people who I interact with on a daily basis. This deep sense of joy carries over into my relationships with others. By digging into the silence, I have been able to ignite a flame of loving presence—a space between well-placed logs. I invite you to do the same, as you find your own way as a leader. "A fire grows simply because the space is there, with openings in which the flame that knows just how it wants to burn can find its way" (Brown, 2016, p. 34).

References

Becker, J. (n.d.). The most underrated sound in our society [blog post]. Retrieved from https://www.becomingminimalist.com/silence-is

Bernardi, L., Porta, C., & Sleight, P. (2006). Cardiovascular, cerebrovascular, and respiratory changes induced by different types of music in musicians and non-musicians: the importance of silence. *Heart, 92*(4), 445–452.

Bourg Carter, S. (2013, November 27). The power of silence in leadership [blog post]. Retrieved from https://www.psychologytoday.com/ca/blog/high-octane-women/201311/the-power-silence-in-leadership

Brown, J. (2016). *The Sea Accepts All Rivers & Other Poems.* Bloomington, IN: Trafford Publishing.

Brox, J. (2019). *silence: A Social History of One of the Least Understood Elements of Our Lives.* Boston, MA: Houghton Mifflin Harcourt.

Bunting, M. (2016). The Mindful Leader: 7 Practices for Transforming Your Leadership, Your Organisation and Your Life. Milton, Qld: John Wiley & Sons.

Condon, B., & Hegge, M. (2014). Honoring Silence and Valuing Community: Living Leadership in 21st Century Teaching-Learning. *Nursing Science Quarterly, 27*(2), 111- 116.

Hollis, R (Host). (2019, November 19). Our First-Ever HoCo Fireside Chat with Rachel and Scott Miller. *RISE Podcast with Rachel Hollis*. Podcast retrieved from https://thehollisco.com/blogs/podcasts/rise-podcast-episode-123

Kaplan, S. (1995). The restorative benefits of nature: Toward an integrative framework. *Journal of Environmental Psychology, 15*(3), 169–182.

Nhat Hanh, T. (2015). *Silence: The Power of Quiet in a World Full of Noise*. New York, NY: HarperOne.

Hall, C., Johnson, K., & McColman, C. (2018, September 24). Parker J. Palmer, Part 1: On the Brink of Silence. *Encountering Silence: A Podcast*. Podcast retrieved from https://encounteringsilence.com/parker-j-palmer-part-1-on-the-brink-of-silence-episode-33/

Petch, N. (2016, May 18). Making The Case For 'Silent Leadership' [blog post]. Retrieved from https://www.entrepreneur.com/article/275940

Wall, J. (2014). Finding an Inner Voice through Silence: Mindfulness Goes to College. *Journal of College and Character, 15*(2), 133–140

Weare, K. (2018). The Evidence for Mindfulness in Schools for Children and Young People [pdf]. Retrieved from https://mindfulnessinschools.org/wp-content/uploads/2018/10/Weare-Evidence-Review-Final.pdf

Chapter 7

Learning to be a Leader: Learning to Value Me

Rachelle Savoie

My early journey into leadership was influenced by a lack of confidence that partly arose from previous leadership attempts where I found it difficult to effectively bring together my internal vision and external actions. For example, my internal voice had clarity and passion, and I knew what I wanted to accomplish. I also believed that I was intelligent and that I could achieve my goals if I really wanted to. However, when I attempted to manifest my vision and goals into the external world, suddenly my inner voice and confidence would weaken. When asked to share my thoughts or beliefs, I would speak too fast—or not at all. It was difficult to clearly articulate what I needed to say, and based on these short-comings I questioned my leadership capacity. This lack of confidence was an entrenched pattern. In grade nine, I stuttered through what I believe was an incoherent campaign speech while running for class president. During competitive team sports, I didn't perform as I would have liked to during tough games, and I often believed that I let my team down. These disappointments pushed my desire to be a leader further behind me, and I decided that it felt safer to be a follower.

It wasn't until I worked alongside inspiring educators that I began to witness the type of leader I aspired to be. I admired certain qualities in leaders, such as integrity, clarity and compassion. I was impressed with how they continued to support other educators who were overworked and under-appreciated and yet still had a strong desire to improve their own practice and support student learning. These leaders recognized the daily challenges that teachers faced and took compassionate action to help alleviate some of that stress. Often these actions were small, such as covering a class for a short time so a teacher could plan with their team. Other times they brought in fitness instructors, recognizing that fitness was important for physical and mental health, but difficult to fit in with busy schedules. Although I didn't feel ready to transition to a formal leadership role during this period, my desire to lead was ignited: I wanted to positively impact teachers and students similarly to the inspiring leaders around me.

Entering the world of international teaching combined two passions of mine: teaching and traveling. However, my first posting at an international school left me questioning the effectiveness of some leaders. After observing and experiencing the negative effects of not making decisions based on the needs of students or classroom teachers—as well as the ineffective practice of using rewards and punishment to motivate behaviour—I found my values and beliefs related to student-centred learning were being compromised, and so I took risks and spoke up for what I knew was right for students. As someone who is uncomfortable with confrontation this was difficult, and I know I didn't articulate my thoughts and ideas as clearly as I wanted to. I was proud that I spoke up, however, even though there were consequences such as not receiving a promotion I thought I deserved. This time was difficult, but it was a powerful learning opportunity. I was able to define the type of leader I didn't want to be, and my gaze started turning towards becoming the type of leader I did want to be; a leader whose actions reflected her words and who welcomed all voices.

Thankfully, I had other experiences in international schools that rekindled my faith in leadership. For example, I saw leaders make decisions that were value driven, and students' academic and social wellbeing were priorities. These leaders also saw leadership potential in me that I had not recognized. Within a one-year period at one school, I was promoted to a department head position—even though I was new to the curriculum. They commented on my ability to facilitate discussions, ask important questions and be inclusive. Qualities I wasn't able to explicitly identify within myself. Although I found myself questioning their judgement and falling into patterns of imposter syndrome, I didn't want to let down the people who had entrusted me to take on this role. During this time, I also began to see the unique benefits and challenges that international schools encounter.

An advantage for many not-for-profit international schools is that the majority of student tuition is dedicated to the improvement of student and teacher learning. At my current school, 1.7% of the overall budget is dedicated to professional development. This budget allows for multiple consultants to come to the school to support a variety of areas. For example, in the past year we have had consultants that supported work in Science, English Language Arts, Foreign Languages, Math, and Instructional Coaching, as well as school wide initiatives that utilized multi-tiered supports and co-teaching. Additionally, teachers are allotted an average of $1200 a year to seek out their own professional development.

Research has shown that teachers improve their practice most drastically when professional development is personalized, consistent, applicable, and involves reflection (Kraft & Blazar, 2018). One role that supports more sustainable professional development is that of an instructional coach. The international school I currently work at has an established coaching program, and I have experienced firsthand the power this role has—both for student and teacher learning. Two years ago, an instructional coach position opened up: I applied and was hired. After 11 years of teaching, the timing seemed right to transition from directly instructing students into a different type of leadership position; the fact that it no longer included evaluation also brought relief. I could focus on improving my facilitation skills, develop curriculum, and partner with teachers to enhance their practice.

Although I had some leadership training, I knew I needed to prepare myself better in this new role as an educational coach. I discovered a graduate-level leadership program focused on developing the human connection and learning to lead with heart. This was not a series of courses that focused on administrative and logistical learning. Little did

I realize how transformational this type of approach would be for both my professional and personal lives. It helped me to identify and name the leadership type I was striving to embody: a heart-led leader. This type of leader acknowledges their own and others' value and leads from "an unselfish and genuine concern for the good of others" (Spaulding, 2015, p.2). The next section will overview my journey with the internal and external preparation that I believe is required to lead with heart.

The Inner and Outer Work of Heart-Led Leadership

Initially, I was on a quest to learn how to serve others effectively as a leader. However, in learning to serve effectively, I needed to start uncovering my own identity and values. How could I lead others through a value-finding process if I couldn't yet articulate what my own values were? How could I show compassion for others when I couldn't show compassion for myself? How could I reconcile the gap between my internal and external worlds in order to be an authentic leader?

Part of answering these questions entailed developing a better understanding of myself, and uncovering both my strengths and areas for growth. Through this process, I discovered that I had been on a journey to leadership for a long time. I reflected on all those failed leadership attempts—from my school life to my athletic life— and I learned that I lacked self-confidence and self-efficacy. Although this was not a new realization, digging a bit deeper to clarify who I am (identity) and what matters to me (values), and connecting these to my role as a leader, was a first step.

I value connecting and communicating authentically with others. The work of Jim Knight (2016) helped me improve my conversation skills by teaching me how to listen with empathy, ask open and non-judgmental questions, and find common ground with others. I also developed an ability to help organize my own—and others'—thoughts, and also focus on a person's strengths (Thinking Collaborative, 2018). These skills have been vital in developing the relationships I need to have in order to be impactful in my work, and are foundational in helping me communicate and connect more authentically.

Being a trusting and authentic presence as a leader is also something I value. Although it is an often-overused term, authenticity does embody what it means to know and live by your values. The process of learning to be authentic is ongoing. Articulating and being grounded in my values has supported me in being confident in my actions and in modeling what it means to speak your truth. Choosing words that align with having integrity and asking questions that are compassionate, yet curious, inspires meaningful collaboration; others will take risks and speak what is important to them—what is in their hearts. Coming to shared understandings also involves carefully listening to others, considering multiple perspectives, and trying new instructional practices (Hunt, 2016).

As I further explored my heart as a leader, I uncovered a desire to learn how to show up and speak up with courage and integrity. Both of these qualities are essential for speaking up for what is right, even if it is uncomfortable; I am constantly working towards improving in this area. The work of Abrams (2009) sets out a process to mentally prepare for these conversations, and provides a structure that allows me to be clear and confident in my words and delivery.

I have also found that being compassionately curious helps me better understand myself and the world, particularly if it comes from a place of kindness and respect. As an instructional coach, I work with a wide range of teachers, many who have different styles and approaches. Entering conversations with an open and curious mind leads to powerful learning about others' and their teaching and learning processes. In my role, I am often on the receiving end of frustrations and challenges, often in the form of issues people have with one another or with the institution. It is in these moments that I try to ensure that I am responding in a way that reflects my values. I want teachers to trust me, but I also know I can't engage in toxic conversations. When this happens, I have learned to either redirect the conversation or correct misinformation (Knight, 2016). Although I worry trust may be broken if I don't agree or join in on the negative talk, I have found that if I employ these tactics and show integrity in my responses, I am seen as being authentic and even more trustworthy.

Benefits of Mindfulness Practice

Journaling has become an important practice of mine—one that incorporates mindfulness through writing—in my journey as a heart-led leader. Journaling allows me to make sense of the often ambiguous and undefined role of a coach, and helps me to sort out the obstacles that are thrown my way. It is also a process I use in order to calibrate my values. When journaling, I like to ask myself pertinent questions, such as: Did I display integrity when that teacher shared her frustrations about her colleague? Was I questioning the teacher about her practice in a compassionately curious way or was I passing judgment? Reflecting on questions such as these has been important to check if my actions embody my values or not. This is the space where I can deepen my understanding of my work, and better understand why and how I lead the way I do: "How a leader knows is at least as important if not more important than what a leader knows" (Brown, 2012, p. 561).

As a leader I might think I know what is right, however, unless I take the time to truly understand the process behind decisions, I may not learn how to effectively make decisions. Aguilar (2018) found that "adults who reflected on their practice, considered their personal motivations, and explored the nature and impact of their interactions with those they served reported higher levels of psychological well-being and were more resilient" (p. 187). Reflective journaling is therefore not only impactful for me, but for those I serve as well, as I am more likely to respond to others in a more informed and mindful way.

The process of journaling allows me to listen to my inner self. It helps me discern if I am connecting who I am and what I value to my actions. For most of us, there is a gap that exists between who we are and what we do. This tragic gap, a term coined by Parker Palmer (2013), represents a disconnect; it can be an internal or an external gap. Palmer describes it as "the gap between the hard realities around us and what we know is possible" (2013). Even though we may never close the gap between our ideal self and actions, Palmer (2013) maintains that the important part is to be mindfully aware of where and when we are falling short, which is a first step in helping us create more effective action.

For me, the tragic gap occurs because there is a disconnect between my mind and heart. I may think something should not agitate or frustrate me, yet at times I have an emotional reaction that prevents me from responding mindfully and effectively. One way I have found to close the gap is by tapping into my "wise mind" (Lineham, 1993, p. 214). Lineham (1993) states that a person uses her wise mind when she takes an experience as it is, directly, without grasping, with more openness and insight, rather than solely through intellectual reasoning. The practice of mindfulness helped me develop my wise mind through deep reflection and listening.

Additionally, mindfulness has helped me deal effectively with emotions through the RAIN practice Aguilar (2018) describes, which involves four steps: Recognizing, Accepting, Investigating, and Non-identification (p.185–186). Learning to *recognize* the emotion, *accept* it, *investigate* it, then apply *non-identification* (not taking it personally), has served me in moments when my emotions could impede my thinking and the ability to respond clearly.

When I have more time, I use a visualization technique modeled after The Four-Fold Way (Arrien, 1993). I envision each of my heart's four chambers as having a particular quality: *full, clear, open,* and *strong*. Each chamber plays an important role in my leadership. Is my heart full? I need a full heart in order to have the capacity to share with others. Is my heart clear? A clear heart aligns my values with my actions. Is my heart open? I need an open heart to avoid being ambivalent. Angeles Arrien (1993) suggests, ". . . states of ambivalence and indifference are precursors to confusion and doubt. The answer is to soften and reopen the heart" (p. 40). A strong heart is where I find the courage to have difficult conversations, and the confidence to persevere when work gets challenging and overwhelming. Being mindful allows me to take the time to consider the impact of my actions on myself and others. I cannot act mindfully if I haven't heard, seen, or understood mindfully. Cultivating a mindfulness practice aligns my heart, wisdom, vision, and actions. Without this, I cannot lead with a full heart.

Learning how to listen mindfully has also served me well as a leader. Mindful listening "is a way of building understanding and connection with kindness and compassion" (Brown & Olson, 2015, p. 122). Often in coaching conversations, how a person says something, and the specific words they use, provide insight into the challenge they might be facing. Previously, when I would have heard, 'students can't do that' or 'my students have too many needs and I have too little support', I would sometimes jump to judgments about the teacher. However, now I step back, look at my reaction, and question my biases or judgements. Then I try to dig deeper into the teacher's values about student learning and growth mindset, which, when unpacked through further open questioning, often reveals a vulnerability the teacher feels about not knowing how to actually support all her students, not an actual belief that they can't learn.

International Teaching and Self-Care

International schools are known for their transient working environments, and there can be a great deal of emotion and stress involved in dealing with the uncertainty and constant changes. Although this is true in many environments, things are somewhat more transient in international teaching, as verified by researchers who have found that turnover rates range from 16–19% per year (Mancuso, S. V., Roberts, L., & White, G. P. 2010, Odland, 2007). At my current school, for the 2018–2019 school year we had an unusually high turnover rate of 32%. Decisions to leave a school range from effectiveness of leadership, better salary and benefits elsewhere, a desire to live in different parts of the world, and repatriation (Mancuso, Roberts & White, 2010, Odland, 2007). People manage transitions in varying degrees of comfort; for example, some teachers have never lived overseas, and some have been living abroad for their entire lives. In my role as an instructional coach, I have an advantage of seeing change both administratively and through the eyes of the teachers. To support a community of constant change, the right conditions are needed. The final section of this chapter is devoted to recommendations that I believe are necessary for heart-led leaders to apply in order to effectively manage a culture of change in international schools.

It is becoming rapidly apparent that self-care needs to be explicitly addressed in many schools. Many teachers I know are inherently self-motivated but also self-critical. They desire to do their best for their students and themselves. As well, the emotional work needed to support teachers is often glossed over or not addressed at all. Emotions are heightened when people are living away from family and friends in an unfamiliar culture, and this can prohibit a person's ability to perform her best. Coaching for effectively managing emotions is an area where the work of instructional coaches can be truly impactful. Leaders at all levels need to develop an effective level of emotional intelligence in order to help others identify their emotions, understand triggers, and to be mindful of how to process and respond to them appropriately. In high stress environments, the ability to be emotionally resilient, avoid over-committing, and knowing how to draw boundaries can be compromised (Aguilar, 2018). Instructional coaches can support teachers in identifying these gaps and provide ways in which to cope. Because coaches work more closely to teachers than many administrators, they also need to be trained to identify burnout, validate these feelings, and coach teachers to respond to them effectively (Aguilar, 2018).

There have been several situations where I thought I was walking into a coaching conversation about planning a unit, but instead ended up listening to a teacher's anxiety about feeling overwhelmed—and in some cases about challenges in their personal life. I was thankful that the teachers were comfortable enough with me to share their feelings. This provided me with the validation that the trust-building work we did fostered positive relationships and openness. Instructional coaches can create the time and space to process challenges, and are an important element for fostering emotional resilience in teachers.

Modeling emotional resilience and self-care is also imperative for supporting teachers. This needs to go beyond providing a mindfulness expert for an afternoon of professional development. A culture of self-care needs to be developed in order to sustain teacher wellness. This requires an openness to discuss emotions; the positive ones and the challenging ones. Brene Brown (2018) has done extensive research into the work of vulnerability and supporting people in identifying boundaries that need to be set in order to attend to their emotions. She provides many resources coaches can use with teachers to tune in mindfully to their emotions. One exercise that I have found valuable is developing my personal emotional vocabulary and literacy to support teachers in naming their emotions (Brown, 2018, p.22). Beyond supporting teachers, that vocabulary is often the key to better understanding an emotional state you are in, and then you can work on alleviating the impact the emotion is having on your wellbeing.

A shift in nurturing a culture of self-care will only be transformational if it is part of a concerted effort with all stakeholders in a school community; of course, it is critical that enough *time* is provided. Some successful models that I have experienced that provide the needed time for self-care include providing a set time within a week where teachers can schedule the meetings they think are most pertinent. By providing more autonomy for teachers to create their own meeting schedules, they will feel trusted and empowered to attend to their needs. Other ways I have seen schools prioritize self-care is having professional development days dedicated to self-care in which teachers can choose from a variety of self-care activities. Another approach is to offer free counselling sessions for teachers to talk to professionals about the stress and anxiety they may be feeling. Removing the financial barriers to some of these services allows more people to access them. As well, administrators organizing these services must keep in mind the challenges of teachers' schedules and provide accessible time within their teaching day. When we begin to honor the time needed to meet the needs of self-care, it is more likely to become achievable.

Conclusion

My journey into developing effective leadership skills took me to many more places than I had anticipated. Exploring and developing the resources of the heart has uncovered an inner desire to be a leader, and has helped define the type of leader I strive to be—a leader that works alongside teachers and students in a compassionate and authentic way. My initial inquiry into leadership has exposed me to invaluable internal and external resources that I can now access in order to build on my strengths and begin attending to my weaknesses. It has also allowed me to recognize the value I have to offer and gain the confidence within myself to serve others. It now feels a lot safer to be a leader, as I am protected by the compassion and wisdom of the heart.

References

Aguilar, E. (2018). Emotional Resilience: The Missing Ingredient. *Educational Leadership*, (75), pp. 24–30. Retrieved from http://www.ascd.org/publications/educational-leadership/may18/vol75/num08/ Emotional-Resilience@-The-Missing-Ingredient.aspx

Aguilar, E (2018). *Onward: Cultivating Emotional Resilience in Educators*. San Francisco: Jossey-Bass.

Arrien, A. (1993). *The Four-Fold Way: Walking the Paths of the Warrior, Teacher, Healer, and Visionary*. San Francisco: HarperSanFrancisco.

Brown, B (2018). *Dare to Lead Read Along Workbook*. Retrieved from https://daretolead.brenebrown.com/workbook-art-pics-glossary/

Brown, B. C. (2012). Leading Complex Change with Post-Conventional Consciousness. *Journal of Organizational Change Management*, 25(4), 560 – 575. DOI: 10.1108/09534811211239227

Brown, V., & Olson, K. (2015). *The Mindful School Leader: Practices to Transform Your Leadership and School*. London, UK: Corwin Press.

Crawford, M. (2009). *Getting to the Heart of Leadership: Emotion and Educational Leadership*. London: Sage Publications.

Hunt, C. S. (2016). Getting to the heart of the matter: Discursive negotiations within literacy coaching interactions. *Teaching and Teacher Education*, (60), pp. 331–343. DOI: 10.1016/j/tate/2016/09/004

Kotter, J. P. (2012). *Leading change*. Boston, Mass: Harvard Business Review Press.

Kotter, J., & Loveerme Akhtar, V. (2019). Charting the Course – The Path to Transformation in Education. Retrieved from: https://www.kotterinc.com/wp-content/uploads/2019/03/Transformation-in-Education-we b-version.pdf

Knight, J. (2016). *Better Conversations: Coaching Ourselves and Each Other to Be More Credible, Caring, and Connected*. Thousand Oaks, CA: Corwin, A Sage Company.

Kraft, M., & Blazer, D. (2018). Taking Teacher Coaching to Scale. *Education Next*. Retrieved from https://www.educationnext.org/taking-teacher-coaching-to-scale-can-personalized-training-become-standard-practice/

Linehan, M.M. (1993). *Cognitive-Behavioral Treatment of Borderline Personality Disorder*. New York, NY: The Guilford Press.

Mancuso, S. V., Roberts, L., & White, G. P. (2010). Teacher retention in international schools: The key role of school leadership. *Journal of Research in International Education*, 9(3), 306–323. DOI:10.1177/1475240910388928

O'Neill, P. (June 1, 2010). *The Heart of Leadership*. Retrieved from http://extraordinaryconversations.com/thought-leadership/2013/7/17/the-heart-of-leadership

Odland, G (2007). *An investigation into teacher turnover in international schools*. Seton Hall University Dissertations and Theses (ETDs).

Palmer, P (2013). *Parker Palmer on Standing in the Tragic Gap*. Retrieved from http://www.couragerenewal.org/723/ Thinking Collaborative. (2018). *About Thinking Collaborative*. Retrieved from http://www.thinkingcollaborative.com/about/

Chapter 8

Igniting *ahcahk iskotew* (spirit fire)

Angela Sanregret

A leader who leads with love knows how to be and live through establishing an authentic connection to herself and to others. Cultivating this authentic connection involves *ahcahk* (spirit) and *iskotew* (fire), which in Cree means *spirit fire*. Spirit fire is located within ones inner self, and is tied to true identity and heart, which empowers a person, and gives them the strength to bring medicine and gifts into the world. My own journey has been complicated and long, but overall beneficial in developing as a heart-led leader. As a principal in a small, rural community, learning how to lead with heart has taught me how to honor my authentic identity and self; this has allowed me to lead others in my building with love and authenticity, assisting them as they develop and cultivate their own *spirit fire*, and connect to what is important in their own hearts. This chapter will overview how I learned to reclaim and ignite *ahcahk iskotew,* and how it has benefited myself and others in my role as a school leader.

My Journey

The journey as a heart-led leader has been informed by new perspectives as an Indigenous woman, educator, and leader. As an Indigenous woman, my *ahcahk* (spirit) has a history of being vulnerable; stifled by the effects of colonization that include systemic racism and oppression engendering a loss of language, culture, spirituality, traditions, and belief systems (Aboriginal Healing Foundation, 2006). I became acutely aware of this as a beginning teacher, when I was full of self-doubt and inner conflict, and it continued until I eventually transformed into a colonized leader in a system where I felt I did not belong. As a teacher, I tried to honor the need to keep my heart open and allow my experiences and relationships with others to enrich and guide me through my learning. However, I realized that the educational system (largely composed of senior leadership personnel from the dominant culture) expected us to suppress our true feelings and thoughts. In essence, I was trained to ignore, detach, and become a robot disconnected from my body, mind, and heart. Fortunately, my humanity recognized that I was not *made* this way, and I questioned this approach—privately, to begin with at least. Unfortunately, because these colonized ideals had suppressed my voice for so long, I felt there was something wrong with *me*, and I did not feel empowered to speak up. This way of being took its toll, and sometimes in despair and confusion I took breaks from the education profession, just so that I could return to a place within myself that felt more authentic, a place filled with *ahcahk iskotew*—spirit fire.

My Indigenous Journey

The journey to reconnect to *ahcahk iskotew* has been ongoing; however, in recent years I began to explore and honor my Cree roots and identity. I am a Métis *iskwew* (woman), but I was not raised with any sense of who I am as a Métis person. My childhood consisted of a typical upbringing in a colonized society. We were a middle-class family who lived in town, attended Catholic Mass on Sundays, and we did not struggle socio-economically. My father's side of the family, the Métis side, spoke French and English at home. However, my grandfather, when imbibing too much alcohol, would speak a language known to us as *gibberish*. Later I learned he was speaking fluent Cree. This was the first time I realized that we were part Cree, and I began to ask questions. However, my family continued to deny this part of my heritage, even as I asked my questions, and I was left on my own to seek out the truth.

Eventually, I found some answers. My best friend is a Cree *iskwew* from Saddle Lake Cree Nation, and she taught me some of the Cree language, culture, and ceremony. I was drawn to her knowledge of our traditions and I spent a lot of time at her house on weekends, learning the language, attending ceremonies, and learning how to smudge. I slowly stopped attending Catholic mass as I started to feel a stronger pull towards Indigenous teachings and ways of being that spoke more authentically to my heart. This withdrawal from the church was natural, and took place before I fully realized the complex history of the Indigenous people and the role of the Catholic Church in the oppressive colonization process against us. Journeying into my Métis and Cree heritages, I began to fill a spiritual hole in my heart. I started to reconnect to my authentic Spirit fire: I felt like I did as a child; full of light and hope, but with a deeper connection to who I am, as a person and a woman. I spent more time looking inward and developing a more encompassing identity that involved my Indigenous heritage. I also had many questions, and I felt confused on how to find my way as an educator and leader in the dominant culture.

Although I began to feel reconnected to my heart and spirit through reconnecting with my Indigenous identity, I had a difficult time finding a place for these important aspects in my work in the public school system. I suffered from burnout trying to be someone I was not. I also didn't believe that there was a place to allow my Indigenous heart to show up in a system tailored to white, middle-class values. After twenty years of working in the public educational system, mostly in Indigenous communities, I felt as though I had little impact on students, parents, colleagues, and the community. However, I had a glimmer of hope that I might be more empowered through a master's degree, which could open doors to leadership positions and allow me to make a bigger impact; I hoped it would also help to decolonize some of the structures, beliefs, and actions inherent in public school systems. For me, decolonizing education involves a mind shift; one where I do not need to follow a specific set of ideals to facilitate learning. In a decolonized approach, all people feel valued and reciprocate learning, and I could see myself being part of this shift as a leader.

Training to be a Leader: Learning to Be Me

When I was accepted into the master's program, I enrolled in a four-course topic within the inter-disciplinary graduate program entitled, *Indigenous Education: A Call to Action*. The first year solidified my passion for learning about the history and legacy of residential schools, the process of decolonization, and how I fit into the important work ahead for Indigenous people. I learned about *Métissage*, a belief that values how different ideas and concepts can be woven together to create strength and change, offering a focus on a system more connected to traditional ways of knowing and a relationship to the land. I began to realize that my heart belonged with traditional Indigenous and Métis teachings, not the colonized approaches to education I had experienced.

Although these initial experiences with post-secondary studies on my way to becoming a leader were positive, they were also difficult. It was hard learning the truths about the history of Indigenous peoples in Canada, and the shaming of my family's heritage through social and political means. I was angry that the colonized history I was taught in the public schools was inaccurate, and even more so it actively contributed to the negative, biased, and racist attitudes towards Indigenous people. In fact, I observed some of these impacts upon myself and the other Indigenous students I went to university with. I could see that we often hesitated to speak in class, to stand up for our beliefs; there was an overall sense of trepidation and feeling that maybe we did not belong in the post-secondary setting. I felt that I was not cut from the same cloth as my classmates and colleagues, and I had a persistent gnawing in my gut and heart that parts of the education system followed a political agenda that still contributed to the socialization of oppressive beliefs, actions, and Indigenous identities. I did not want to be a part of this agenda, and the need for authenticity and relevancy in my studies and my path as an Indigenous woman leader grew stronger.

During the second year of studies, I chose the *Leading with Heart* program, which I hoped would cultivate my leadership identity in a more authentic way. Something deep within me (maybe *ahcahk iskotew*) let me know that leadership was the path for me, but how to bring in Spirit fire was another matter. As I entered the Leading with Heart classroom I had very few expectations, aside from some of the titles of the readings that used words such as *Heart-Led* and *Mindful*. I began to think that this program may not be the traditional leadership training I was usually exposed to. As I sat in a circle with a group of 18 others, I felt a bit uneasy, but intrigued. Indigenous people traditionally work in circles. We use talking circles to discuss problems, to have important discussions or debates, or to obtain oral traditional knowledge, which meant that fortunately I was comfortable with this method of teaching and learning.

Although I was a bit anxious at the beginning, the two week on-campus portion of the program turned out to be a transformative process. Through the purposeful teachings of mindfulness practices, within a framework of uncovering authentic self, vision, and path, I embarked on a journey that was also supported by my classmates. The nature of the program meant that we developed particularly strong bonds; because of these bonds, I felt safe and dove deep into my inner being. I came up to the surface learning how to accept and love myself just as I am, including learning how to process uncomfortable emotions of pain and grief, that were in part, bound to the effects of colonization.

Mindfulness practices were an important part of this learning process. I learned how to become more aware of the present moment, and how to put some distance between myself and thoughts that were quite simply just *thoughts*—not who I was as a person. Through mindfulness practices such as RAIN - Recognize, Allow, Investigate, and Non-Attachment (Brown & Olson, 2014), I learned to bring compassion to difficult emotions, which when attended to can provide new insights. I felt myself getting stronger in my mind and heart as I learned to become a more emotionally intelligent leader through sitting, "…with our sadness, pain and insecurity" (Bunting, 2017, p. 32), and then letting it go. Mindfulness, as well as a safe community of peers, created a space for me to learn from what was arising in myself, and learn how to deal with these thoughts and emotions in *skillful* ways.

The results of the growth and development I experienced was also evident in my work life. I had obtained a principal position in a new school on a Métis settlement in rural Alberta, and I was both nervous and excited for this new path. I wondered if I would find success as an educator in a colonial public school system. Questions swirled around me: *Would working in a provincial system create new experiences related to loss of my Indigenous identity and authentic self?* I had many doubts. Before I began my cultural explorations, I left the provincial system feeling like I was not a good educator or leader, and that my indigenous heart did not belong. When I worked in the federal system, in the reserve-based school, I felt more of a sense of belonging. However, now I was back in the provincial system once again, and I wondered if I had the personal fortitude and leadership skills to enhance the teaching and learning for both staff and students.

Through becoming reacquainted with my heart, Indigenous teaching, and inspiring knowledge keepers, I have made much progress as a heart-led leader. My professors from the University, elders from the communities I worked in, and the numerous new friends I made through my cohorts, provided valuable insights and wisdom, which I began to weave and integrate with my own personal wisdom. Through Cree ways of knowing and being, I learned to trust myself, have faith in the Creator, and take part in more opportunities for ceremony. This also includes the integration of mindfulness practices with Indigenous teachings. For example, I realized that I honor the present moment when smudging. Smudging helps me calm my mind and express gratitude for life and the land that I am blessed to walk upon. The practice of smudging renews my focus and keeps me grounded in an authentic and centered heart that guides my career, my connections to people and the earth, and life in general. I have learned to appreciate the land and what it provides for me, such as plant medicines, the healing spirit, and the guidance of animals and the natural elements. I realize that all beings are my relations and they are instrumental in making me who I am as *iskwew* (woman). Being mindful is a natural way to notice and appreciate these things.

Reclaiming Spirit Fire

Developing a strong and authentic self and identity, partly through embracing and bringing healing to my Indigenous identity, and partly through applying mindfulness practices to skillfully build emotional intelligence, was important for me as a new leader: this development impacted my ability to lead others in exploring and strengthening their own identity and self. Central to this is learning how to acknowledge one's *ahcahk iskotew*, or spirit fire. Through exploring spirit fire, a person knows their gifts, fire, or *spark*, which Benson (2007) describes as a part of the self that longs to be named and put into the world: a spark, a light that helps people come alive, that comes from within and provides "a prime source of meaning, self-directed action, and purpose" (Benson, 2007, p. 19).

Helping others find their spirit fire can be daunting; after all, this is not common work we do every day with our teachers and students in the public school system. In my work as a principal, I have purposefully provided opportunities for my staff to explore spirit fire through reflection and contemplation, such as through offering a daily meditation communicated through emails, and through opening spaces at staff meetings for reflection, discussion, and activities related to wellness. I have also facilitated self-care challenges for individual staff members, and, when appropriate, we have reviewed their experiences upon their return to work.

One of these activities consisted of inviting staff to create a *spark* board, a visual display a person's uniqueness gifts and passions, which speaks to things that have heart and meaning and their expression in the world. For example, our school secretary took up the challenge and created her spark board using a collage consisting of her family, her gifts and talents (such as her interests in horses), along with pictures of other activities she loved doing. She communicated that by creating her spark board she was better able to identify her natural interests and gifts, and how honoring these things made her feel more joyful and connected to others. The other staff members, however, did not respond to this challenge. The feedback I received was that they did not know *how* to explore their spirit fire or spark. Additionally, in the past, staff was not supported to engage in non-curricular activities or talk about and display individual pursuits and interests. However, I believe I am changing my school culture through modelling how to explore one's spirit fire, by talking to staff about my own process, breaking things down so they can take small steps, and creating a safe and accepting learning community, which is foundational for trying new things. However, this takes time.

Mindful Listening and Communicating

As a principal, I am learning to open my heart, utilize mindful listening, and become consciously aware of my biases and assumptions (Brown & Olson, 2015, p. 116). Learning to listen without judgement takes practice, especially during encounters when I feel irritation, such as when staff complain about the behaviors of others. Although this is challenging, I practice being mindful in the moment so that the other person feels attended to and heard. I still notice when I am irritated by what is being said, but I focus on listening to the essence of what I hear people communicating. It is their moment to be heard; I do not need to be in my head thinking what to say next in order to *correct* the other person, or even offer them advice. I've also learned that I can maintain my connection to people even though I may not agree with them, and that to begin any process people really need to be heard first.

Developing effective communication skills has been a challenge as a principal, especially during difficult conversations. I am learning to courageously hold the space for people to talk about their thoughts and ideas, to help others feel heard and understood, which naturally leads to resolving or transforming a situation for the better. However, it is a difficult thing for me to refrain from *fixing* or wanting to be a hero—to allow the conflict to resolve with patience, silence and processing time (Brown & Olsen, 2015, p. 123). After difficult conversations, I have also found the phrase, "So what, now what," to be helpful in reinforcing the importance of acknowledging issues and then moving toward their resolution (Cliatt-Wayman, 2015, n.p.). Using this phrase with teachers, as a guiding principle, is really useful when someone is stuck in rehashing a problem or situation. I also find that it helps to reframe mistakes as opportunities for learning, and applying that learning in the future. It reminds all of us that we are human, and that we keep learning and growing from one situation to the next.

I also extended the use of the *so what, now what* idea with students, reminding them of their ability to take responsibility for their feelings, beliefs, and actions, and how this empowers them to be able to do something in a situation they might feel powerless about. One way I model this is by mindfully listening to a student with patience, and without judgement, and then simply thank them for sharing, then asking: *What now?* After doing this process with one student, he told me that it sounded like in the future he probably needed to *mind his own business*, and I laughingly agreed. Through this process of listening and communicating with the ear of my heart (Arrien, 1993), we take the time to listen and accept our own and others' thoughts and feelings, acknowledging that they are worth being listened to. These are actions that facilitate caring and self-justice, particularly for people whose voices have been systemically oppressed.

The Importance of Story

Honoring stories through the process of listening to one's journey brings insight and wisdom. Traditionally, in the Cree culture, educating others is done orally through stories. We are taught that everything that *is*, has a story. Every living being has its own story and is part of a journey. I believe that my journey as a leader contains my story and purpose, and the reader has peered into a small part of this. By telling and re-telling my story through the years, I learn to understand my own self with compassion and wisdom. Through this process, I know that my forty-five years on the planet has led me to exactly where I am today as a heart-led leader, particularly when I started to listen to the story of my heart and the roots of my Indigenous background.

Similarly, my staff and students also have their own stories and journeys. Those stories should be honored and heard, as they reveal who each individual is and what makes them who they are. Each person has their own gifts, experiences, and knowledge, and I want these to be evident in our school culture. The opportunity for celebrating and sharing collectively comes during our Monday assemblies, where as a school body we listen to what students did on the weekend. This often leads to other conversations—both between staff and students and between students alone—that reveals who they are as individuals and what they value in their lives. When someone finds the courage to share something with another person, they are often telling us what is important in their lives. These stories need a place to be heard and witnessed.

Another way I honor students' stories is when they are sent to my office. I mindfully communicate with them and learn more about who they are while helping them resolve their problems. For example, one student broke down when he was telling me about how another student was bullying his brother, who has a muscular myopathy. He told me how he was struggling trying to be friends with this boy, but how difficult it was when this person is mean to his brother and he feels so angry. He has learned through our conversations how to deal with this anger in a positive way, and he has now had heart-to-heart conversations with the other student, which made him feel less angry and more confident in managing his emotions. He told me the story of his anger and how he deals with it, and also other important factors, such as his struggle to deal with his mother's volatile and aggressive reactions to anger. I also shared my stories with anger, and those of my own children, letting him know that learning how to deal with anger is a skill; happily, he kept practicing with grace and maturity. These types of open and authentic conversations are more beneficial than just passing judgment and dishing out punishment.

Listening to the stories of staff members is also important. Daily, I try to have open conversations regarding how things are going at work or in their lives. I visit teachers in their classrooms and actively engage staff in conversation about their children, their homes, their parents and grandparents, and their hopes and dreams. As a heart-led leader, I approach people and situations with openness and acceptance, and I help to create an accepting space through having an open-door policy and authentically listening to the stories of others. My staff often comment as they leave my office a bit lighter: "thanks for listening" or "thanks for your understanding."

A school is made up of many different people, with varying personalities, complexities, and issues. I try to enact mindful listening and understanding of people's stories, which often leads us to seeing something insightful; it could be recognizing a way forward or perhaps taking the steps to end an old story or start a new chapter. Sometimes a person just needs space and time to process or cool down, and both students and staff know my office is a safe place for this. I work extra hard at building relationships and connections within the school and community. The way we are together reminds me of a metaphor related to the parts of a tree. A *mistik* (tree), with all its *watihkwan* (branches), needs to be nurtured, as the health of one part impacts the health of the whole. Additionally, some parts of the branches break off, so that new parts can grow, similar to when we take a different path and start a new chapter in our collective story. We are all part of the whole tree, connected through a trunk that grows and thickens with time. But we also all have our own individual *mistik* metaphor about our individual stories, and it is up to me as the leader to facilitate this story-gathering and story-telling process in my school. As a principal, I need to honor others' stories, a process which supports the reconciliation process: stories are a powerful force that challenges and resists domination (Graveline, 1994, p. 45), and are vital to Indigenous voices or others' voices that have been lost or unheard.

Self-Care

An important part in my role as a leader is taking care of myself, which means addressing and nurturing my need for safety, satisfaction, and connection (Hanson, 2018, p. 37). I cannot create a healthy learning space in my school if I do not consider and care for these important human needs for me first. In the past, I took little time for myself and consequently felt stressed, experienced burnout, and took breaks from work to regain some peace and balance, which is a sporadic and non-sustainable intervention. Sometimes, I tell myself that I don't have enough time for self-care, or that I am too tired. At other times, my self-care consists of me sitting in front of the TV, eating unhealthy snacks, and not exercising.

Since becoming a principal, however, I've learned how to practice self-care geared to my needs and I incorporate small actions each day to feel resourced and connected to myself and others. For example, to unwind after work I practice mindful meditation, play piano, play word games with family, and go for walks in nature. Every morning before I get into my car to drive to work, I take three deep breaths and say *nanâskomowin*, which means *I am grateful to the Creator*. These cleansing breaths mentally prepare a space for the day in my head and heart and remind me of my strength. I also smudge with sage daily to cleanse any negativity I might be harboring. I find it helpful to pray for others and to allow myself to feel grateful for my life. Scheduling a massage once a month has become a part of my self-care regime. I believe that I have the right to be healthy and well, and I have intentionally made efforts to find small, yet resourceful, ways to look after myself.

Principal as Rock

The natural teachings that come from rocks have also informed acts of strength building, self-care, and empowerment as a leader. Since beginning my graduate studies, I have developed a stronger connection to the natural world, and particularly with *asiniy* (rocks). Rocks for me hold both knowledge and spirit. They remind me of my strength and ability to be stable and provide a safe place to address my own needs, as well as the needs of others. Rocks are found in a variety of forms, ranging from majestic mountains to tiny pebbles to grains of sand between my toes—and each of these forms have something to teach me. For example, the sand between my toes that feels soothing and relaxing reminds me to let go and allow myself to remain grounded by finding ways to relax my mind and body. The pebbles that sometimes get stuck in my shoes and cause irritability and pain remind me to take the time to look after the hard and messy things that need to be dealt with—that's it not OK to keep walking around with a rock in my shoe.

Additionally, huge rock formations or mountains remind me that rocks take up space, without hiding behind other rocks or trees. I too must remember to not shirk or hide my true self or abilities as a woman or an Indigenous person, but in fact honor my birthright to take up space in the world: I am here, I exist, and I have value.

As a leader, I am a rock for myself and for the members of the school community. Rocks also allow for ideas and experiences to either bounce off them or, with enough repetition, to flow over them, transforming them over time. Rocks also hold fire. They remind me of the fire within myself and others, and the need for creating a space to allow our passionate gifts to burn brightly, providing light for each other. The silent rock reminds me to be still and reflect as the sun goes down on the day. *Have I done a good job today? Did I practice mindful listening with that staff member who was struggling? Was I authentic and intentional in my interactions with the people around me? Have I appreciated the new ideas that were shared?* I am not striving to be perfect, but I am striving to be better. Each day I can become more effective through remembering to engage the teachings from all of the aspects of my life, which informs and broadens the resources for connection and my heart.

As I cultivate a decolonized space for myself and others, I am guided by a vision of *ahcahk iskotew (spirit fire)*, that helps to unleash healthy energy for myself and others. I am grateful for the knowledge I have gained from my fellow travelers as a heart-led leader, along with the reassurance that *I am* a leader and that I have an important place in the education system. I have gained many gifts through reconnecting with my Indigenous roots and my human heart, which has been facilitated through intentional formational practices within my graduate training programs. Along with the spiritual guidance provided by ceremony and the Cree ways of knowing, I feel strong on my path, like a rock, but also continuously transforming and changing, embraced by my *ahcahk iskotew*.

References

Aboriginal Healing Foundation, (2006). *Final Report of the Aboriginal Healing Foundation: Promising Healing Practices in Aboriginal Communities* (Volume III). Ottawa, ON: Aboriginal Healing Foundation. Retrieved from: http://www.ahf.ca/downloads/final-report-vol-3.pdf

Arrien, A. (1993). *The Four-Fold way: Walking the Paths of the Warrior, Teacher, Healer, and Visionary*. New York, NY: HarperOne.

Benson, P. L. (2007). *Spark: How Parents Can Help Ignite the Hidden Strengths of Teenagers*. San Francisco, CA: Jossey-Bass.

Brown, V., & Olson, K. (2015). *The Mindful School Leader: Practices to Transform Your Leadership and your School*. London, UK: Corwin Press.

Bunting, M. (2016). *The Mindful Leader: 7 Practices for Transforming Your Leadership, Your Organisation and Your Life*. Milton, Queensland, AU. John Wiley & Sons.

Cliatt-Wayman, L. (2015). *How to fix a broken school? Lead fearlessly, love hard* [Video file]. TEDWomen. Retrieved from https://ted.com/talks/linda_cliatt_wayman_how_to_fix_a_broken_school_lead_fearlessl y_love_hard

Graveline, F.G. (1998). *Circle Works: Transforming Eurocentric Consciousness*. Halifax, NS: Fernwood Publishing.

Senge, P. (1990). The Leader's New Work: Building Learning Organizations. *Sloan Management Review, 31*(1), 7–22.

Chapter 9

The Necessity of Self-Care for Professional Survival: Confessions of a New Leader

Amelia Bird

First and foremost, I am a teacher. I truly believe that this is my calling. I feel alive when I'm in the classroom, and helping students provides fulfillment like nothing else in my life. I also believe that all teachers are leaders. Every day we make decisions that impact a group of people, whether students or staff. Understanding the needs and complexities of being a teacher guides my decisions as a leader.

After five years as a classroom teacher, a more formalized leadership role presented itself. It still involves teaching, but in a different capacity; one that also includes leading learning as a technology consultant for a school division in Alberta. Although the role was exciting—and a huge learning curve for me (which I enjoy)—I found myself becoming drained and unsatisfied because I was so fully immersed in this new learning experience that I forgot to take care of myself. During the second year in this role, I knew I needed to make some changes. I started to feel isolated and lonely, something that has been documented by other educators experiencing burnout (Fabian, 2013). It was at this time that I began to see a need to invest in my professional and personal self-care. I began reading material that fostered personal growth, journaling, meditating, and I also focussed on connecting with others who were on a similar journey in order to share strategies. I was able to use my newly acquired mindfulness skills to improve my quality of life, at least for a while.

Very recently, I accepted a new position as acting director of technology. This was an unexpected honour, for two main reasons: I am at the earlier stages in my career as an educator, and I am a woman. To preface this, whenever I attend technology conferences the majority of the representation in technology leadership is men. Additionally, until recently in our division much of the senior administration consisted of men, and a culture that existed that was often referred to as *the old boys' club*. In the K-12 education profession, the majority of employees are female, yet district office staff typically contains a much higher percentage of men (Hoff, Menard, & Tuell, 2006). I am fortunate to work in an area where this cultural norm is changing. I am also so grateful to have a strong mentor in my former director, the first female director of technology in our school division.

The role of a director involves working with people in many different departments within a school division to promote system wide change. I need to know our divisional policies and best practices to guide my work and decision making. I also need to have knowledge of our technology platforms and the work that needs to be done to keep our systems running and schools functioning as efficiently as possible. A solid understanding of the operations of our school division and the responsibilities of our department is also required, but gratefully I don't need to know how to troubleshoot every hardware and software issue; for that I have others on my team with various areas of expertise who can help out.

Being responsible for the day-to-day operations of the technology department is a humbling experience. We are living in an age where technology is evolving more rapidly than ever before. I am constantly learning from the members of my team, as each person has a unique skill set and history of how we have done things in the past, which can be important information to move forward! Every day presents a new challenge or mystery to solve. Sometimes I know the answer quickly, other times I need time to investigate and learn. I am learning to be kind to myself when I don't know the answer right away. What I am learning is that although I don't know everything, I care enough to find out—and this means a lot to the people that I serve. Also, I have learned that although I deal with a lot of emails, there is much value to the human connection facilitated by calling people on the phone or visiting them to learn more about how we can help.

Moving into this role has opened my eyes to the complexities that come with being viewed as a leader. Margaret Wheatly (2008) discussed the feeling of being on the edge, and I connect with this on several levels. She said, "Today, most of us walk that edge between hope and despair, trying not to look down for fear of losing our footing" (Wheatley, 2008, p. 44). This resonates with me; I used to think that leaders had all of the answers and confidence. There are days when I feel full of hope and enthusiasm in my role, and other days that are filled with despair. It is certainly a bit of blind faith that keeps me going each day.

One of the key pieces of wisdom I have learned as a leader is understanding that all of the answers are not readily accessible. Sometimes I have to make a decision, only to find that if I had other pieces of information I might have made a different decision. This happens to me on a daily basis. The only way I can take comfort in this is in viewing each of these decisions as a resource to draw upon when making future decisions. As a former people-pleaser, it has been a bit of a struggle to get over the fact that I will not be liked by everyone all the time. Sometimes I have to have honest conversations with people, and these conversations are instrumental in moving relationships forward or not.

As mentioned earlier, with regards to the gender balance especially, I acquired this leadership role at a very pivotal time in my current school division. For many years, our central office team consisted of mostly men, and we are now in a place where our central office team is composed of more women in leadership roles than ever before. I am fortunate to be a part of this team, and also to have strong female mentorship to help me navigate the unknown. Although I have always had strong female mentors, and consider myself a strong female, a lot of people that I have viewed in positions of power have been men. I am now able to find mentorship and learn from the female leaders around me. I am also empowered to believe that it is possible to be considered for leadership positions and that there is not a gender prerequisite. In a previous teaching role, I noticed that administration was always only men; beyond that, any time that someone had to fill in for administration a man would be asked. I felt that this was a potential barrier in my career as the possibility for growth and leadership never seemed to be granted to women. In the section below, I will discuss some of the tensions I have encountered as a new leader, and how I used a heart-centered approach to find effective resolutions. My own sense of personal justice has grown because I have been given an opportunity to show my leadership as a result of the dedication that I have demonstrated to my profession, as well as through the relationships that I have fostered in my professional community.

The Constant Tension

My new role has had many challenges, and I can relate to the following quote, "Sometimes we balance precariously on the edge of burnout. It takes courage to lead in the face of so many challenges" (Centre for Courage and Renewal & Francis, 2018, p. 4). One of my main challenges is that I often feel like I'm a fraud, that I don't belong in this role. In starting a new role, it is difficult to let go of the fact that I don't *know it all* yet. However, I have learned that humility can help me stay grounded in knowing that I will probably *never* know it all—in any role. I'm also grateful to have a team of people who hold space for me. This work would be impossible to do without advocates. One of my biggest advocates is the person who had the role before me, and I'm so fortunate to be able to reach out to her for guidance and advice. It is also comforting to have someone to bounce ideas off of and know that there is no judgement.

An interesting piece of my emerging leadership experiences is in learning how to hold the tensions when they arise, and when to push back ever so gently. As someone who likes to please others and works hard, I have been guilty of taking on tasks that are not mine. Because I sometimes want to be a *hero*, I sometimes take on much more than I can handle as a way to prove myself. As Wheatley and Frieze (2010) put it, "It is time for us to give up these hopes and expectations that only breed dependency and passivity, and that do not give us solutions to the challenges we face" (p. 1). In order for teams to work effectively together, each member has to be able to be open enough with the other team members to share their experiences, history, successes, and defeats in an effort to move forward as a more productive unit.

Thus, showing that I do not have all the answers is actually an asset. However, the question that I must ask myself is: "Why do I think I have to prove myself more than others?" When I reflect upon this (often by taking a long walk to enjoy some fresh air), I think that perhaps I feel a bit of the *imposter syndrome*. However, I then reflect on the fact that I pursue my work with integrity and always try my best, and that is all I can offer: my best. The more I learn about my role, and the role of others on my team, the more I am able to appreciate distributed leadership. I am part of a team of people who have incredible skills, and I need to help my team do their best work—and expect equal accountability from each person.

Leader as Host

Wheatley and Frieze (2010) reiterate that "Leaders who journey from hero to host have looked beyond the negative dynamics of politics and opposition that hierarchy breeds, they've ignored the organizational charts and role descriptions that confine people's potential" (p. 31). I would not be able to be in my position if I didn't have a team of people whom I could count on. I have learned that although I am acting director of technology, I do not necessarily know how to solve every problem that comes my way. I need to have a team to bounce ideas off of, and to have problem solving conversations with, to move forward. It is important for me to know the skillset of my team and to know when and to whom to reach out to when I need help.

I have also been learning about the art of hosting conversations. Learning how to ask someone questions to help the person become self-reflective allows them to be empowered in solving their own problems; it has been a wonderful addition to my leadership toolkit. I have found this to be very empowering in staff meetings, as it allows each member of the team to provide input and suggestions instead of simply being told what to do. This helps with staff buy-in when introducing new initiatives and helps staff feel like valued, contributing members of the team.

Communication Needs Appreciation

People need to be appreciated. Sometimes in the fast pace of the school environment, we forget to take time to thank our colleagues for their efforts. I have found that taking time to thank members of my team who go above and beyond, whether at a staff meeting or in a group email, is a nice way to recognize the efforts of the people we rely on each day. In acknowledging our colleagues, we have a brief moment to connect and remind them of how important they are to the organization. Considering the amount of time that people spend at work, I think it's important to increase positive interactions with our colleagues to help meet the natural human need of being valued, appreciated, and cared for.

Each member of my team has their own set of hopes, dreams, stressors, and strengths. I try to honour and recognize my team members and show compassion in times of need. I think that it is important to check in with my team members to see how they are doing. We spend so much time at work, it is important to know that our colleagues are looking out for us. I try to express gratitude to my colleagues, especially when they take on more than is expected of them for the benefit of the team.

Holding My Seat

There are difficult days and difficult situations in my role. There are days when I think that I'll have to resign because I simply can't take the pressures anymore. There are times when I am in a position where I have to make decisions that will not be favourable to others. It is disheartening and never easy to do. I try to remember Chodron's (1998) advice where she suggests that when times are tough, I connect with the heart and see obstacles as teachers. In my work, this often shows up as being blamed when things are not working perfectly. When you are the leader, the blame comes down heaviest on you. In order to connect with the heart and see obstacles as teachers, I have to remind myself that as a team we will come up with a solution, and we will use the experience to be proactive in the future.

I also relate to Chodron's (1998) advice that in difficult situations, one must, "hold their seat" (n.p.). I often visualize being on a wild stallion and hoping with all my might that I won't fall off the horse. Through learning to sit with anger, disappointment, and confusion I have learned that I will indeed survive, and maybe even learn something worthwhile. In my work environment, I have learned that sometimes it is best to wait for a period of time before replying to difficult emails. Giving myself a chance to collect my thoughts and cool down has always been beneficial. Chodron (1998) wrote, "Each time you sit still with the restlessness and heat of anger—neither acting it out nor repressing it—you are tamed and strengthened" (n. p.).

Palmer (2011) also described a similar process, one that provides personal strengthening through "holding tension in life-giving ways" (n.p). In the past, I have been guilty of avoiding or trying to dispel tension as quickly as possible. However, in leadership, as in life, there will be tension. When working with others, there will be tension. It is how I perceive and work with the tension that matters. For example, there are many complex problems that our technology team is faced with, and it is easy to want to resolve a problem quickly. However, as I have come to learn to manage tension, I have found that sometimes the best solutions are found by sitting with the tension for a while.

Believe That Everyone is Doing Their Best

I have found that when working with an array of people, sometimes we can get frustrated with each other. The root cause is almost always lack of communication. It is usually a case of people having information that they assume you know, and therefore don't think it necessary to share, followed by misinterpretation and lack of understanding or missed deadlines, which leads to further frustration. I have learned that it is important to ask questions. A lot of questions. I try to view situations from different angles and ask questions to help me get to the root of the issue. It helps me be a more effective learner and problem solver.

Self-Care

The work in education never stops, but that doesn't mean that people should not take some time to step away from the constant demands and pressures. In a world where we can be connected twenty-four hours a day to—and through—technology, it is easy to think that I should always be tied to my cell phone and email. In fact, I nearly burned myself out in the first year of teaching because I didn't set proper boundaries with technology. One thing that I have learned is that other people won't necessarily tell you where that line is. You need to set your own boundaries and be ok with them. This was one of the greatest gifts that I have given myself. Giving myself permission to unplug in the evenings and on weekends has allowed me to feel more energetic and fulfilled, both at work and in my personal life. The other piece to this is not feeling guilty about not being tied to your work or device all the time, even though it was admittedly difficult.

Part of my role as acting director of technology is to teach people how to have a healthy relationship with technology, staff and students alike. As someone who is an advocate for technology, I am also aware that it should not be all consuming. As a leader, I play a part in conveying mindfulness when it comes to technology usage. According to Growing Up Digital, Alberta (2018), "More than half of Alberta teachers feel that digital technologies are a negative distraction in their own lives" (n.p). It is also extremely important to address "digital rights and responsibilities" (Ribble, 2012, p.150), as often our students do not feel the same ethical pressures in the digital world that they may be aware of in the real world.

Another component to my self-care in a highly demanding position is to have a strong network of people that I trust and can reach out to when needed. It is important to have trusted colleagues that you can collaborate with on the many complex problems. Much of the work in the technology department is intertwined with other departments, so I need to have connections with many people across the school division. The work is much more enjoyable when I take the time to foster relationships with my colleagues. In fact, I have taken the time to get to know people across our entire division, including their strengths and expertise, and this helps me with problem-solving in collaboration with some great minds. As well, it collectively allows us to work together for the betterment of others, which is instrumental in helping work feel like a place where people find meaningfulness and connection.

I am also very grateful to my family and friends: they support me unconditionally and help me take time to do things that I enjoy outside of a stressful work environment. I have learned that when work is the most stressful, that is when you need to take time to do something that you enjoy. I often walk my dogs, and this stress relief works every time. I find anything active outdoors is good for my soul. Music also helps to relieve tension, and I rely on it constantly.

It is important to move beyond the lip service of wellness in the workplace and actually model and help others to achieve it. I have noticed that if I have an off week at work, my lack of energy and enthusiasm can spread to the rest of the team, and then we are not functioning optimally. Bunting (2016) states that, "Leaders set the tone for the whole team or organisation: when they are calm, confident, open and relaxed, the team is more likely to feel the same. Likewise, when they are stressed, fearful and closed, it breeds the same emotions among team members" (p. 1). Wellness can look different for different people; however, it is important that I know what each member of my team needs in terms of wellness, and that I communicate my needs to my supervisors as well.

I also very much appreciate and aspire to Bunting's (2016) definition of mindful leadership: "Mindful leadership means deliberately cultivating a state of wellness and being a beacon of goodness, responsiveness and clarity, even in the toughest circumstances" (p.1). I use this on my email signature line as a constant reminder that this is what I am striving for. I will never have all of the answers, but I am always committed to doing my best for students and my colleagues. As I did in my classroom as a middle and high school teacher, I want to be responsive and kind to all beings, and help them address their needs, even in the toughest circumstances. In creating strong, supportive working communities, I believe that my team and I will be more fulfilled, appreciated, and have the space to dream and create like never before. The work is always going to be challenging, but with a willing mindset, some supportive colleagues, friends, and family—and a little blind faith—it is possible. The inner work that I do to enhance myself as a person will be an ongoing endeavour. This work, however, will strengthen my ability to be a calm, compassionate leader who can both hold her seat and hold tension in life-giving ways (CCR & Francis, 2018).

References

Bunting, M. (2016). *The Mindful Leader: 7 Practices for Transforming Your Leadership, Your Organisation and Your Life.* Milton, Australia: Wiley.

Center for Courage & Renewal & Francis, S. L. (2018). *The Courage Way: Leading and Living with Integrity.* Oakland, CA: Berrett-Koehler.

Chodron, P. (1998). *Holding Your Seat When The Going Gets Rough.* Retrieved from: https://www.lionsroar.com/holding-your-seat-when-the-going-gets-rough/

Fabian, J. (2013). *Moving Forward; Sitting Still: An Auto-ethnographic Study of Mindful Educational Leadership.* Doctoral Dissertation.

Growing up digital (GUD) Alberta. (2018). Retrieved from https://www.teachers.ab.ca/SiteCollectionDocuments/ATA/About/Education%20Research/Promise%20and%20Peril/COOR-101–10%20GUD%20Infographic.pdf

Hoff, D. Menard, C. & Tuell, J. (2006). Where are the Women in School Administration? Issues of Access, Acculturation, Advancement, Advocacy. *Journal of Women in Educational Leadership, 4*(1), 43–63.

Palmer, P. (2011). *Five habits of the Heart.* Retrieved from: http://www.couragerenewal.org/habitsoftheheart/

Ribble, M. (2012). Digital Citizenship for Educational Change. *Kappa Delta Pi Record*, *48*(4), 148–151. doi: 10.1080/00228958.2012.734015

Wheatley, M., & Frieze, D. (2011). It's time for the heroes to go home. *Leader to Leader*, *2011*(62), 27–32. doi: 10.1002/ltl.489

Wheatley, M. (2008). An Era of Powerful Possibility. *The Nonprofit Quarterly*, 44–46. Retrieved from https://nonprofitquarterly.org/an-era-of-powerful-possibility/

Conclusion
Living With Heart: Self-care, Collective care, and Justice

Amy Burns

Leading with heart, as a concept, is one that has surfaced in recent years in a multitude of professional areas including business, education, religion and so on. In his work as a leadership speaker and former CEO, for example, Tommy Spaulding (2015) speaks of heart-led leadership as a philosophy that will "change your life, your organization, and the lives of everyone you touch. And if you do it right, it will change the lives of everyone they touch" (pp. 1–2). As a practice and a way of conceiving of leadership, leading with heart offers the opportunity for leaders in vastly different pursuits to gather under the umbrella of leadership, not of others, but for others. Indeed, it presents to us the chance to live with heart, both for ourselves as leaders and for those with whom we work. As has been demonstrated in the chapters contained within this volume, living and leading with heart can be personal and it can be collective. Regardless of the impact, however, living and leading with heart is an act of social justice that holds the promise of belonging for all.

Living with Heart: Self-care as Social Justice

In my own leading with heart journey, as I came to better understand the theoretical foundations that had always underpinned my leadership philosophy, it became clear that I had neglected the role of self-care. Focused solely on collective care and the wellbeing of others, my leadership did not attend to my own needs and I believe I saw this as a positive thing, as a sign of service to others, however this was in error. In modeling self-care for those with whom we work, we are promoting a form of social justice. In doing so, we both legitimate the time that self-care takes as important and valuable work while also demonstrating qualities of grit and resilience.

As has been demonstrated in this volume, self-care is not just about the self, but about impacting others through the self (see in this volume, for example, Cameron, 2020; Chrol, 2020; Seaman, 2020). In taking the time for self-care, leaders legitimize the time this requires and open spaces for those they work with to practice self-care also. Cherkowski and Walker (2018) describe the criticality of this when they note that "teachers, just like all persons in all kinds of work, need and deserve environments that will support them in ensuring they can attend to self-care so that they may thrive in their work" (p. 23). And indeed, within education specifically, the self-care and resultant wellbeing of teachers is intricately linked to the wellbeing of students. This is not the sole domain of education however. Where leaders make time for self-care and allow this to be modelled to those with whom they work, others are likely to follow, ensuring every person they interact with sees the positive results of self-care also.

While creating the time and space for self-care is critical to ensuring others feel empowered to engage with their own needs also, leaders also have a role to play in demonstrating the results of that care. This, too, is an act of social justice because when we employ our own wellbeing for the betterment of others, there are increased opportunities for others to do the same. Perhaps nowhere is this more apparent than in the development of grit and, as a result, resilience as a leader. Hanson (2018) describes grit as "dogged, tough resourcefulness. It's what remains after all else has been ground down" (p. 77). It is inevitable that all people, be they leaders in formal positions or those who look to them, will experience challenges and obstacles (see, in this volume, for example, Bird, 2020). What is not inevitable is the way in which we respond. Leaders, in difficult times, have the opportunity to model strength, described by Hanson as *agency*, described as one being "active rather than passive, taking initiative and directing your life rather than being swept along. Agency is central to grit, since without it a person can't mobilize other internal resources for coping" (p. 78). Modeling this way of living with heart, of promoting self-care to develop grit and the ability to mobilize internal resources in times of stress, these are critical ways leaders can create the spaces for people to develop strength and lift themselves up.

Living with Heart: Collective Care as Social Justice

Collective care is a clear road to elements of social justice as it is what allows us to raise one another up. But to look at care generally is to perhaps miss the nuanced opportunities we hold as leaders to ensure those we lead go on to lead others in a caring way. Compassion and flourishing are two terms relate closely to discussions of collective care and they matter in all areas of professional life. Although often relegated to the helping professions such as healthcare and education, collective care is critical to ensuring the health and success of those we, be it in the boardroom or the classroom.

Worline and Dutton (2017) outline the importance of compassion in the workplace, noting that "without compassion, workplaces can become powerful amplifiers of human suffering" (p. 11). This stark description paints a clear picture of the role of compassion in social justice for without compassion, leaders may be contributing to what seems for some a hopeless endeavor. Worline and Dutton go on, however, to discuss the many ways leaders can ensure a culture of compassion exists, termed compassion moves. "While in the grind of time, organizations grip us with task demands, deadlines, and performance pressures, compassion moves buffer us and create spaciousness to awaken our capacity for compassion even as we keep work going" (p. 90). Integrating compassion into our work as leaders allows us to create capacity for compassion. It allows us to support communities of people who support one another in the pursuit of collective wellbeing (see, in this volume, for example, Sanregret, 2020; Savoie, 2020).

In addition to compassion, or perhaps as a result of it, flourishing is also a concept discussed with regard to collective care. In education specifically, the ideas presented around flourishing tend to describe, in one way or another, school culture and the role that this plays on both teacher and student wellbeing. In describing a participant in their research, Hibbert et al. (2018) told the story of Karen, an educational leader determined to provide the conditions for understanding necessary for flourishing. To this end, Karen described that "she needed to ensure that her teachers had what they needed to enjoy being with their students" (p. 43). In this statement, there was a recognition that joy and fulfillment would lead to greater things. Karen also went on to highlight the role of the school culture and community in this work.

She also recognized that in order to support her teachers, she needed to look after her own wellness. She found her own support through the strong educational assistants, teacher leaders, school council members, and other principals she worked with. She wondered whether better understanding different people's roles and responsibilities might be fruitful. (Hibbert et al., 2018, p. 43)

In this story, Hibbert et al. provide for us an illustration of the role of collective care and understanding in schools that flourish. The concept of flourishing, however, is not one relegated to education alone. Spaulding (2015) noted of caring in response to organizational success:

> When you care for someone of something, whether a child, a client, an employee, or a potted plant, you want to see it do well. Too many leaders see caring for others as a sign of weakness. In reality, caring is all about strength. It takes strength to champion a purpose beyond profits, to step out of the spotlight, to support the vision of others, and to inspire them to find and follow a purpose. (p. 82)

As Spaulding shows us, collective care and the support of all takes leadership strength and compassion.

How Leading with Heart becomes Living with Heart: A Summary

The chapters that you have read within this volume have described the leading with heart journeys of various people in various personal and professional contexts. As noted in the introduction, the chapter authors presented here undertook a program that asked them to consider their leadership practice as a part of their wellbeing and the role of that practice on the wellbeing of others. What we learned, and what has been chronicled here, is the way in which that leading with heart journey became a living with heart journey.

In the summer of 2018, our inaugural cohort was welcomed into the program and would spend one year with us doing four courses in this important leadership topic. No one could have imagined what would occur. Much as one would expect from such a program, students were exposed to various leadership authors who attended to the human element (see, for example, Caza & Jackson, 2011; Novak, 2009; Spaulding, 2015; Starratt, 2009; Worline & Dutton, 2017). There was also significant and purposeful attention put on the role of mindfulness for leaders themselves and for those they lead in their work (see, for example, Brown & Olson, 2015; Hanson, 2018). Indeed, in that first summer that marked the beginning of the leading with heart course, and in many respects my own leading with heart journey, students engaged with theory and literature each morning and practiced mindfulness and connection in the afternoons. Students were invited to see the role of their own wellness in the wellness of others and the impact that this could have on the collective vision of their organizations, be they schools or businesses. They were encouraged, as leaders, to consider what it means to stay in the moment, knowing that, as leaders who face moments of stress personally or who work with those in moments of stress, it is "harder to stay mindful when things are stressful or emotionally demanding" (Hanson, 2018, p. 23). To say that they became connected to one another would be the definition of understatement. They still gather today to connect with and support one another. They now live with heart, supporting one another.

The Leading with Heart program is now getting ready to welcome it's third cohort, and while the program has changed and morphed in response to the needs of its participants, the core remains the same. It is about leading compassionately. It is about helping to support people in their personal and professional contexts so that those people can be well and healthy and go on to do amazing things. It means many things but for the contributors in this volume, a common thread being the way in which leading with heart has impacted the way in which they live their lives. Their leading with heart journeys have become living with heart journeys and have allowed them the understanding to impact the living with heart journeys of others along the way.

PS: As I sit putting the finishing touches on this piece of writing, which has drawn themes from the authors included in this book as well as underscore the importance of this topic, I am struck by the timeliness. I am writing from home as the COVID-19 pandemic has washed over us, moving my entire faculty to work remotely, continuing to serve students and move initiatives forward in a brave new way. Never before has leading and living with heart been so important.

References

Brown, V., & Olson, K. (2015). *The mindful school leader: Practices to transform your leadership and your school.* London, UK: Corwin Press.

Cameron, J. (2020). Self-care, conflict, and the path to wholeheartedly embracing leadership. In A. Burns & M-A. Mitchell-Pellett (Eds.), *Leading with heart: Enacting self-care, collective care, and justice* (pp. 47–58). Burlington, ON: Word and Deed Publishing.

Caza, A. & Jackson, B. (2011). Authentic leadership. In A. Bryman, D. Collinson, K. Grint, B. Jackson, & M. Uhl-Bien (Eds.), *The Sage handbook of leadership* (pp. 352–364). London, UK: Sage.

Cherkowski, S. & Walker, K. (2018). *Teacher wellbeing.* Burlington, ON: Word and Deed Publishing.

Chrol, R. (2020). Heart beats: Finding a rhythm of self-care in education. In A. Burns & M-A. Mitchell-Pellett (Eds.), *Leading with heart: Enacting self-care, collective care, and justice* (pp. 33–46). Burlington, ON: Word and Deed Publishing.

Hanson, R. (2018). *Resilient: How to grow an unshakable core of calm, strength, and happiness*. New York, NY: Harmony Books.

Hibbert, K., Rodger, S., Bates, P., Hellerman, K., Ott, M. & Rodger, M. (2018). What would it take to bring joy backinto the lives of teachers and students? In S. Cherkowski and K. Walker (Eds.), *Perspectives on flourishing in schools* (pp. 37–52). Lanham, ML: Lexington Books.

Novak, J.M. (2009). Invitational leadership. In B. Davies (Ed.), *The essentials of school leadership (2nd edn.)*, (pp. 53–73). Thousand Oaks, CA: Sage.

Sanregret, A. (2020). Igniting ahcahk iskotew (spirit fire). In A. Burns & M-A. Mitchell-Pellett (Eds.), *Leading with heart: Enacting self-care, collective care, and justice* (pp. 107–120). Burlington, ON: Word and Deed Publishing.

Savoie, R. (2020). Learning to be a leader: Learning to value me. In A. Burns & M-A. Mitchell-Pellett (Eds.), *Leading with heart: Enacting self-care, collective care, and justice* (pp. 95–106). Burlington, ON: Word and Deed Publishing.

Seaman, D. (2020). Vulnerability as self-care. In A. Burns & M-A. Mitchell-Pellett (Eds.), *Leading with heart: Enacting self-care, collective care, and justice* (pp. 19–32). Burlington, ON: Word and Deed Publishing.

Spaulding, T. (2015). *The heart-led leader: How living and leading from the heart will change your organization and your life*. New York, NY: Crown Business

Starratt, R.J. (2009). Ethical leadership. In B. Davies (Ed.), *The essentials of school leadership (2nd edn.)*, (pp. 74–90). Thousand Oaks, CA: Sage.

Worline, M.C. & Dutton, J.E. (2017). *Awakening compassion at work: The quiet power that elevates people and organizations*. Oakland, CA: Berrett-Koehler Publishers Inc.

About the Authors

Debra Seaman is a teacher and learning leader who focuses on mindfulness practices in both her classroom and leadership work. Gardening, hiking, baking, and reading all allow Debra the time and space to engage in her own mindfulness practice, keeping her grounded and connected.

Rob Chrol is an educator and professional learning facilitator in Manitoba, Canada. He holds Bachelor degrees in both Music and Education as well as a Master of Educational Research. He is passionate about exploring connections between self-awareness, neuroscience, and authenticity-based approaches to leading and learning.

Jacqueline E. K. Cameron is on a perpetual mission to not be bored but to find opportunities for creativity and connecting. She's working on saying what she means, and meaning what she says as she navigates parenthood, teaching, academia, and finding every chance for adventure and learning with her family

Kimberley Dart is a manager at the University of Calgary and an ardent supporter of career development and student success. She is a devoted life-long learner. Kimberley lives in Calgary, Alberta, with her husband, son, and two cats. Her crowning achievement is her ability to fold fitted sheets.

Lisa Talbot is an instructional leader and teacher in Calgary, Alberta. As a graduate student at the University of Calgary's Werklund School of Education, life-long learning is at the heart of her vision. Lisa focuses on wellness in learning, leading, and teaching. She loves to spend time with her family.

Katie McIntyre is a teacher, student, wife, momma, writer, and all-around kind human being. She participated in the inaugural year of the Leading with Heart program and embraced Silence as a life-long companion. Katie lives in Airdrie, Alberta, with her husband Dan and son Dexter.

Rachelle Savoie is a Canadian expat who has taught internationally for 10 years. She has embarked on a life-long journey to understand her inner and outer worlds better. She lives in Dubai with her husband and their lively 1-year-old, who teaches her something new every day.

Angela Sanregret is a Métis mother of four. She is a principal and writer, and has almost completed a three-year Masters' program. She is dedicated to the decolonization of education. Angela lives with her children in Elk Point, Alberta.

Amelia Bird began her career teaching math and science in rural Alberta. For the past three years she has been an educational technology lead teacher for her school division, assuming the role of acting director of technology. She is finishing her Masters of Education at the University of Calgary.

About the Editors

Dr. Amy Burns is an Associate Professor and Associate Dean, Undergraduate Programs in Education with the Werklund School of Education, University of Calgary. Amy's current research focuses on the development of systemic thinking and leadership competencies in preservice and early career teachers as well as the impact of school leader collective wellbeing and resilience on teachers and school vision. Amy is co-creator and Academic Coordinator of the Leading with Heart graduate program with the Werklund School of Education at the University of Calgary.

As a public-school teacher, counsellor, school-based administrator, **Dr. Mitchell-Pellett** has effectively created spaces where people learn to acknowledge their inner gifts and resources in service of changing cultural narratives that better empower the self and others. She researches and implements approaches that facilitate the vertical and horizontal development of pre-service teachers and leaders, including how mindfulness practices impact the development of qualities of being essential to teacher and leadership formation. She is co-creator and instructor of the *Leading with Heart* program at the University of Calgary's Werklund School of Education. As a trained facilitator in the Circle of Trust© process based on the work of the Center for Courage and Renewal, she enjoys creating shared spaces where important intersections between the individual and community can join to inspire and transform change from the inside-out. Mary-Ann is a district consultant for new teachers and emerging leaders in Manitoba, where she also facilitates arts-infused mindfulness workshops, and loves spending time in nature on the shores of her home along the beaches of Lake Winnipeg.

Manufactured by Amazon.ca
Bolton, ON